MODERN NOVELISTS

General Editor: Norman Page

MODERN NOVELISTS

MODERN NOVELISTS

ALBERT CAMUS

Philip Thody

St. Martin's Press   New York

First published in the United States of America in 1989

Printed in Hong Kong

ISBN 0-312-02055-4

Library of Congress Cataloging-in-Publication Data
Thody, Philip Malcolm Waller, 1928–
Albert Camus.
(Modern novelists)
Bibliography: p.
Includes index.
1. Camus, Albert, 1913–1960 – Criticism and
interpretation. I. Title. II. Series.
PQ2605.A3734Z7369   1989   848′.91409   88–4444
ISBN 0-312-02055-4

Contents

Acknowledgments

I am grateful to Hamish Hamilton for allowing me to quote from translations of Camus's works.

Annette Torode typed the many versions of my manuscript with exemplary care and good humour. Gwilym Rees made his accustomed and invaluable contribution to the accuracy and readability of what I had written. Any mistakes are entirely my own.

My thanks also go to the British Taxpayer who provided the customary one hundred per cent subsidy without which this book – like my others – would never have been written.

General Editor's Preface

The death of the novel has often been announced, and part of the secret of its obstinate vitality must be its capacity for growth, adaptation, self-renewal and even self-transformation: like some vigorous organism in a speeded-up Darwinian ecosystem, it adapts itself quickly to a changing world. War and revolution, economic crisis and social change, radically new ideologies such as Marxism and Freudianism, have made this century unprecedented in human history in the speed and extent of change, but the novel has shown an extraordinary capacity to find new forms and techniques and to accommodate new ideas and conceptions of human nature and human experience, and even to take up new positions on the nature of fiction itself.

In the generations immediately preceding and following 1914, the novel underwent a radical redefinition of its nature and possibilities. The present series of monographs is devoted to the novelists who created the modern novel and to those who, in their turn, either continued and extended, or reacted against and rejected, the traditions established during that period of intense exploration and experiment. It includes a number of those who lived and wrote in the nineteenth century but whose innovative contribution to the art of fiction makes it impossible to ignore them in any account of the origins of the modern novel; it also includes the so-called 'modernists' and those who in the mid and later twentieth century have emerged as outstanding practitioners in this genre. The scope is, inevitably, international; not only, in the migratory and exile-haunted world of our century, do writers refuse to heed national frontiers – 'English' literature lays claims to Conrad the Pole, Henry James the American, and Joyce the Irishman – but geniuses such as Flaubert, Dostoevsky and Kafka have had an influence on the fiction of many nations.

Each volume in the series is intended to provide an introduction to the fiction of the writer concerned, both for those approaching him or her for the first time and for those who are already familiar with some parts of the achievement in question and now wish to place it in the context of the total *œuvre*. Although essential information relating to the writer's life and times is given, usually in an opening chapter, the approach is primarily critical and the emphasis is not upon 'background' or generalisations but upon close examination of important texts. Where an author is notably prolific, major texts have been selected for detailed attention but an attempt has also been made to convey, more summarily, a sense of the nature and quality of the author's work as a whole. Those who want to read further will find suggestions in the select bibliography included in each volume. Many novelists are, of course, not only novelists but also poets, essayists, biographers, dramatists, travel writers and so forth; many have practised shorter forms of fiction; and many have written letters or kept diaries that constitute a significant part of their literary output. A brief study cannot hope to deal with all these in detail, but where the shorter fiction and the non-fictional writings, public and private, have an important relationship to the novels, some space has been devoted to them.

NORMAN PAGE

To Gunther Kloss

1

The Man, the Books and the Themes

Albert Camus was born on 7 November 1913, at Mondovi, a small town in the Bône district of Eastern Algeria. His father, Lucien Auguste Camus, was an itinerant vineyard worker, who had learned to read and write in the orphanage where he had spent his childhood. Camus's mother, *née* Catherine Sintès, could not sign her name on her marriage certificate. She remained illiterate to the end of her life.

On 11 October 1914, Lucien Camus died in a military hospital of wounds received during the first battle of the Marne. A fragment of shell found in his body was sent back to his widow. She kept it, next to his photograph, on the wall of the small apartment to which she now returned in her native city of Algiers.

Camus had an elder brother, Lucien, born on 20 January 1909. Catherine Camus, now aged thirty-one, was untrained for any profession. She worked for a time in an armaments factory, before becoming a charwoman. Either through shock at the news of her husband's death, or as a result of an attack of meningitis, she was slightly deaf. Her younger son was later to write of her that she 'found thinking difficult'.[1] Never, according to the semi-autobiographical essays *L'Envers et l'endroit* (*Betwixt and Between*), published on 10 May 1937, did she hug or caress him, for 'she did not know how'.[2] In his *Carnets*, the working notebooks which he began to keep in May 1935 but which were not published until after his death, he wrote: 'I loved my mother with despair. I have always loved her with despair.'[3]

While his mother went out to work, Camus and his brother were looked after by their grandmother, Catherine Sintès. *L'Envers et l'endroit* presents her as a harsh, selfish woman, much given to play-acting in order to make people sorry for her. She was

1

accompanied, at least in the early years of Camus's childhood, by two of her sons, Etienne and Joseph. The apartment, in the rue de Lyon, on the edge of what was then the European working-class district of Belcourt, had three rooms. When the family wanted to eat, they moved the bed out of the room occupied by Etienne and Joseph and put up a table. There was no running water, and no bathroom. The only artificial light was provided by an oil lamp. There were no books.[4]

On 16 October 1957, Albert Camus was awarded the Nobel Prize for literature. He was the ninth French writer to win it, and the youngest. Only Rudyard Kipling, who had been honoured in 1907, at the age of forty-one, was younger at the time of the award. Camus dedicated his Nobel Prize speeches to Louis Germain, the Primary School teacher who had given him the coaching and encouragement without which, as he recognised, he would not have won the scholarship that enabled him, in 1924, to go to what was then the Grand Lycée d'Alger.

The normal path for a clever boy like Camus would have been to do as D. H. Lawrence had done some thirty years earlier in England and become a schoolteacher. But in December 1930, at the age of seventeen, Camus fell ill with tuberculosis. It was a bad attack, and he lost a lot of blood. In his second book of essays, *Noces (Nuptials)*, published on 23 May 1939, he noted down what may well have been the doctor's own words: 'You are strong and I have to tell you the truth: I can tell you that you are going to die.'[5] The apparent imminence of his death made an understandably dramatic impact on him. The whole of what he himself called the 'first cycle' of his work, the books published between 1937 and 1944, is dominated by the idea of physical mortality. The tuberculosis which almost killed him in 1930, and which was to recur at intervals throughout his life – in January 1942, in the winter of 1949–50 after his visit to South America, in 1957, after the award of the Nobel Prize – made it impossible for him to enter a profession in which he would be in daily contact with young people.

Camus nevertheless went on to study at the University of Algiers. In 1936, he successfully presented a *Diplôme d'études supérieures* – roughly the equivalent of an MA thesis – on St Augustine's reading of the second-century Greek philosopher Plotinus. This still reads as a competent if slightly derivative piece of work, and has the advantage of enabling critics who share

Camus's agnosticism to observe that he did know something about the Christian beliefs which he rejected.

The first entry in Camus's *Carnets*, made in May 1935, stated that 'one can, with no romanticism, feel nostalgia for lost poverty'. He had already, at the age of seventeen, left the apartment in the rue de Lyon and gone to live with his uncle, Antoine Acault, a fairly wealthy butcher of strongly Voltairean persuasion. Camus kept himself alive by selling spare parts for motorcars, working as a clerk in the Préfecture d'Alger and as a research assistant in a meteorological survey of the Sahara. He turned down Antoine Acault's suggestion that he should ensure himself both a comfortable income and plenty of time in which to write by becoming a butcher. In 1934, he further annoyed his uncle by marrying Simone Hié, the daughter of a fairly wealthy ophthalmologist. The marriage, which lasted only two years, was not a success. It ended with Camus's discovery that his wife, a morphine addict, was sleeping with one of his friends in order to obtain money to buy drugs.

None of Camus's mature works bears any obvious traces of his poverty-stricken early childhood or of his fairly tumultuous adolescence. In 1943 he wrote in his *Carnets* that he had spent ten years acquiring something which he thought priceless, a heart free from bitterness,[6] and he never lost the memory of having been poor. His first completed novel, *La Mort heureuse* (*A Happy Death*), written between 1936 and 1938 but not published until 1971, eleven years after his death, dwells in some detail on the advantages of being rich. In 1947, in a lively exchange of public letters with the left-wing journalist Astier de la Vigerie, Camus observed that he had discovered freedom not in the works of Karl Marx but in poverty.[7] But at no point did he set out to write the French equivalent of D. H. Lawrence's *Sons and Lovers* or of George Orwell's *Keep the Aspidistra Flying*. Neither did he try to offer his readers a twentieth-century parallel to the novels in which the nineteenth-century rebel Jules Vallès described his struggle against the poverty of his early childhood. His three major works of fiction – *L'Etranger* (*The Outsider*, 1942), *La Peste* (*The Plague*, 1947), *La Chute* (*The Fall*, 1956) – are all what the French call 'les romans de la condition humaine', novels of man's fate. They are interesting for the ideas they express and the way in which the stories are told. If they do talk about Camus's private life, it is to illustrate a general point about man's nature and situation. Each of the books undoubtedly presents the way in which he saw the world at the time he was writing it. Each of them forms part of an intellectual autobiography. They are rather like the essays and novels of Aldous Huxley: the account of how one man tried to make sense of his own experience.

Camus tried to discourage critics from seeing his books as reflecting his own private experience. While he did not go so far as George Orwell in expressing the wish that no biography should be written of him, he would probably have been surprised at the success of Herbert Lottman's 750-page biography. Unlike authors such as Gide or Proust, he had never set out to use his private life as a source of his literary work. Camus also insisted, especially in the later part of his short life – he was killed in a car accident on 4 January 1960, at the age of forty-six – on the fact that he saw himself primarily as an artist, concerned first and foremost with questions of composition, presentation and technique. If it is not always easy to remember this, and if critics have tended to concentrate on the content of his books rather than on their form, it is partly Camus's own fault. The topics he treats, the characters he creates, the problems he discusses and the issues he raises are so interesting that you tend to forget that the books he wrote are also works of art. It is a little like Pascal's remark that you expected to meet an author and find a man. This, undoubtedly, helps to explain why his books have proved so popular. Readers like seeing how other people try to make sense of their experience. It helps them to understand what is happening to them. When the glimpses they catch of the man behind the books reveal a personality like that of Camus, it is not surprising that they should want to know more about him.

There are other ways in which Camus's view of himself does not wholly coincide with the qualities that make him so fascinating a writer. Throughout his life, he was intensely interested in the theatre. In 1935, in company with a group of friends, he set up the Théâtre du Travail at the newly created Maison de la Culture at Algiers. This passion for the theatre never left him, and in January 1960, at the time of his death, his 1959 stage adaptation of Dostoevsky's *The Possessed* was on tour in northern France. His enthusiasm for Spanish revolutionary syndicalism led him to write, in 1935, a play called *Révolte dans les Asturies*. The authorities in Algiers, for fairly obvious reasons, refused to allow it to be performed, but it was published as an 'essai de création collective' (an attempt at collective creation). Appropriately enough, in the light of this later insistence that the suffering of the innocent made the Christian idea of God totally unacceptable, one of the major parts he played in the theatre in Algiers was that of Ivan in his own production of *The Brothers Karamazov*. He also adapted André Malraux's pro-Communist *novella Le Temps du mépris* (*Days of Wrath*), and played the part of Christy Mahon in the French version of Synge's *The Playboy of the Western World* which the Théâtre de l'Equipe, the successor to the Théâtre du Travail, put on in 1939.

It was also for the Théâtre de l'Equipe that Camus wrote his own play *Caligula*, completing a first version in 1938 and having the pleasure of seeing it produced in Paris in 1945. In 1944, he explored a particularly gloomy version of his concept of the absurd in *Le Malentendu* (*Cross-Purpose*) and in 1948 collaborated with Jean-Louis Barrault in *L'Etat de siège* (*State of Siege*), an adventurous work which took up a number of the ideas of *La Peste*. In 1949, he developed an important aspect of his concept of political revolt in *Les Justes* (*The Just*). In the 1950s, he adapted works by Caldéron, Lope de Vega, Pierre Larivey and William Faulkner, and on 12 May 1959, gave an hour-long television broadcast explaining how he was never happier than when working in the theatre.[8]

But for all this enthusiasm, Camus never obtained anything like the success in the theatre enjoyed by writers such as Jean Anouilh or Jean-Paul Sartre. *Le Malentendu* and *L'Etat de siège* were both flops, and although *Caligula* did run for over three hundred performances, it is remembered in theatrical circles largely for the revelation it provided of the talents of the young Gérard Philipe. *Les Justes* also ran for over four hundred performances and, like the 1956 adaptation of Faulkner's *Requiem for a Nun*, did enjoy a *succès d'estime* with the critics. But compared to Sartre's *Les Mains sales* (officially known in English as *Crime passionnel*, 1948), also a play about the problem of ends and means of politics, it is neither very good theatre nor a particularly interesting play about politics.

In 1950, Camus said that he thought of himself as a writer whose works were so closely related to one another that none of them could be fully understood in isolation from the others.[9] This is true of all his books. *La Peste*, in particular, gains considerably from being read side by side with the articles he published in *Combat* and elsewhere immediately after the Second World War.

But Camus's permanent reputation does not rest either on his journalism or on his work in the theatre. It is based on a thousand or so printed pages of lyrical and philosophical essays, of novels and short stories. None of these works is very long. *L'Envers et l'endroit* and *Noces*, taken together, make up just over seventy pages in the second volume of the Pléiade edition of Camus's works, published in 1965. *Le Mythe de Sisyphe* (*The Myth of Sisyphus*, 1942), an essay on the absurd, contains only 112 pages. *L'Homme révolté* (*The Rebel*, 1951), in spite of its ambition to trace the history of revolt from the Greeks to the present day, has only 112 pages. Even when you add the short stories in *L'Exil et le royaume* (*Exile and the Kingdom*, 1957) to *L'Etranger*, *La Peste* and *La Chute*, you get less than six hundred pages of completed fiction, not much more than the length of one major novel by Balzac, Stendhal or Dickens.

From October 1938 until September 1939, Camus worked as a regular member of staff on the newly established left-wing newspaper *Alger Républicain*. This was useful to him in a number of ways. It was his first regular, salaried employment. He was now, however vivid the memories of his childhood, and however sincere his sympathy for the poor and oppressed, a member of the professional middle class. His work as a journalist gave him the opportunity to clarify some of his ideas by reviewing novels, short stories and essays as they came out. His articles on Sartre's *La Nausée* and *Le Mur*, in 1938 and 1939 respectively, are a good indication of the direction his thoughts were taking as he worked on *L'Etranger* and *Le Mythe de Sisyphe*.[10] *Alger Républicain* also provided him with a political forum that was especially useful now that he had left the Communist Party.

He had been a member of the Party from August 1935 to October 1937, when he was expelled because he refused to accept the change in the Party line on the Arab question. The Franco-Russian pact, negotiated in May 1935 by Pierre Laval, had involved some *quid pro quo*s. One of these was that Russia would put pressure on the French Communist Party in order to make it moderate its opposition to French colonialist policies in Algeria and elsewhere. The Party duly obliged, and expelled those of its members who, like Camus, thought that the needs of the Arabs were more important than the strategic interests of the Soviet Union. The strongly anti-colonialist line of *Alger Républicain* gave Camus the opportunity to write about two of the three political issues about which he felt most strongly throughout his life: his hostility to General Franco; and the condition of the Arab population in his native Algeria. His opposition to the death penalty became public only later.

On 19 December 1938, in one of his very first articles, Camus defended the role of the International Brigade in resisting Franco's rebellion against the republican government in Spain. In 1945, in one of his articles in *Combat*, he urged America, Britain and France to exert diplomatic pressure in order to bring down Franco's régime.[11] In 1949, he set *L'Etat de siège* in Spain in order to emphasise that the general criticism of totalitarianism in *La Peste* could be directed to a specific target. In 1952, when Spain was admitted to UNESCO, he resigned from that international organisation in protest, and in March 1957, in an article denouncing the Soviet occupation of Hungary, he specifically compared the establishment of tyranny there to the example of Franco's Spain. He also wrote:

> I regret in this respect to have to play Cassandra again, and to disappoint the new hopes of some of my indefatigable colleagues, but no evolution is possible in a totalitarian society. Terror doesn't evolve, except toward worse, the scaffold doesn't become liberal, the gallows is not tolerant. Nowhere in the world has one seen a party or a man disposing of absolute power not utilizing it absolutely.[12]

It would have been interesting to see how Camus might have behaved after 1975, when Spain began its return to democracy. He might well have joined those who contrasted the speed with which tyranny disappears in the modern world when it is based upon the rule of only one man with its apparent unshakability when fed on an ideology and sustained by a self-perpetuating oligarchy. When it is Hitler, Mussolini, Franco, Salazar or the Greek colonels who stand in the way of democracy, this tends to return when they die or fall from power. It is, in this respect, perhaps a little early to judge whether the reforms introduced by Gorbachev will prove of lasting significance.

Camus's work on *Alger Républicain* on behalf of the nine million or so Arabs who lived side by side, but not on an equal basis, with the nine hundred thousand European settlers in Algeria led him into quite an active form of investigative journalism. Between

January and March 1939, he published a series of articles which helped to secure the release and acquittal of Michel Hodent, a specialist adviser employed by an Arab insurance company, who had been wrongly imprisoned because his attempt to apply the law correctly had annoyed the big French landowners. In June 1939, Camus also published eleven articles describing the devastating effects of the famine then raging in Kabylia. While recognising that this famine was a natural disaster for which nobody could be held specifically responsible, he nevertheless made it clear that the general situation had been made very much worse by the injustice and inefficiency of the French administrative system. He did not, it is true, suggest at that or any other time that the final remedy lay in the establishment of an independent Algeria. This was not an idea which anybody entertained in the 1930s, and it finally became acceptable to the French themselves only in the late 1950s. But Camus had made himself sufficiently unpopular with the French authorities for them to blacklist him for any kind of work in Algeria. *Alger Républicain* closed down at the outbreak of the Second World War, in September 1939, and its temporary successor, *Le Soir Républicain*, which Camus edited in collaboration with Pascal Pia, ceased publication in March 1940. Camus then had to go and work in Paris, where Pia found him a job as a typesetter on the right-wing, mass-circulation evening paper *Paris-Soir*, popularly known as *Pourri-Soir*.

After the outbreak of the Algerian war on 1 November 1954, Camus was widely criticised for his failure to come out openly against the policy of trying to keep Algeria French. In particular, he was attacked for his failure to condemn the use of torture by the French army of prisoners suspected of complicity with the pro-Arab Front de Libération Nationale. He had, it was pointed out, been a member of the resistance movement during the German occupation of France, and there was a widespread view, especially on the left, that the struggle for Algerian independence represented exactly the same values which had inspired the French resistance. This pressure took its most dramatic form on 12 December 1957, when Camus held an informal question and answer session at Stockholm University as part of the events accompanying the award of the Nobel Prize. An Arab student asked him why he had not denounced the torture and terrorism practised by the French army in Algeria. Camus replied:

I must also denounce a terrorism which is exercised blindly, in the streets of Algiers for example, and which some day could strike my mother or my family. I believe in justice, but I shall defend my mother above justice.[13]

It is, perhaps unfortunately, Camus's most famous remark, more frequently quoted than the closing words of *Le Mythe de Sisyphe*: 'The struggle towards the summit is alone sufficient to satisfy the heart of man. We must imagine Sisyphus as happy.' Camus explained elsewhere what he meant, and his position is not an indefensible one. His mother was still living in Algiers, and went to the market every day to do her shopping. If a terrorist had thrown a bomb and killed her, and if the use of torture might have prevented this bomb from being thrown, then Camus would, in some way, have been guilty of her death. The argument presupposes, of course, that torture does help to prevent terrorist acts. Its usefulness is, perhaps, as suspect as the supposedly deterrent effect of capital punishment. In 1958, Camus recognised this very clearly when he wrote, in his *Avant-Propos* to *Actuelles III*, that it 'had perhaps managed, at the cost of a certain honour, to discover thirty bombs, but at the same time produced fifty new terrorists'.[14]

Camus nevertheless first became known to a wider audience not as a result of what he had tried to do in Algeria in the 1930s but through his work as a journalist in the French resistance newspaper *Combat* in 1944 and 1945. The publication of *L'Etranger* in July 1942, and of *Le Mythe de Sisyphe* in October of the same year, had made him well known in literary circles, but it was only with his emergence from clandestinity after the liberation of Paris in August 1944 that he became a national figure. The slogan of *Combat*, 'De la résistance à la révolution' (From resistance to revolution), represented a very widely held view that the successful fight against the German invader ought to lead fairly quickly to a socialist revolution and to the final destruction of the right-wing forces which had collaborated with the Germans and supported the Vichy régime. The articles which Camus published in 1944 and early in 1945 strongly suggest that he shared this opinion. He moved to a more moderate position only when it became evident that such a revolution would lead either to a one-party state of the type which the Russians were establishing at the time in Eastern Europe, or to a violent civil war. In November

1946, the publication in *Combat* of the series of articles entitled *Ni victimes ni bourreaux* (*Neither Victims nor Executioners*) showed that Camus now saw the 'People's democracies' of the mid-1940s as a greater danger to freedom and democracy than the continuation of an economic system based at least partly on the private ownership of property.[15] *La Peste*, which echoes many of the themes of these articles, is imbued with the conviction that left-wing totalitarianism is as evil a force as Hitlerian fascism ever was.

Camus also used his position in *Combat* to try to alert French public opinion to what was happening in Algeria. On 6 May 1945, during the celebration of Victory in Europe Day, a serious riot broke out in Sétif, in the south of Algeria. According to the figures published by the French government, 102 Europeans were killed. The reprisals, again according to French government figures, caused the death of 1500 Muslims. A later parliamentary enquiry put the figure at 15 000.

Between 13 May and 15 June 1945, Camus published in *Combat* a series of eight articles explaining the gravity of the economic and political crisis from which Algeria was suffering. But the French government had other problems on its mind, and an attempt at electoral reform in 1947 was sabotaged by the European population in Algeria. In 1956, Camus wrote regularly in the liberally minded *L'Express*, which had become a daily paper for the purpose, in order to support the electoral campaign of Pierre Mendès-France. He argued in favour of a cease-fire by which both sides in Algeria would agree not to attack the civilian population, of a round-table conference, and of the eventual establishment of a Swiss-type federation.[16] He did not comment on the return to power of General de Gaulle in May 1958, or on the widespread view at the time that de Gaulle might be the only man strong enough to keep Algeria French. The European population in Algeria certainly thought this, and its members were bitterly disappointed when de Gaulle, between 1958 and 1962, performed the apparent miracle of giving Algeria its independence without causing a civil war in France.

By 1962, Camus was dead, and not there to comment on the irony by which a million or so Europeans, until that year inhabitants of what was officially and proudly called *L'Algérie Française*, fled their native country and were welcomed back as 'des rapatriés' (people who had come home). As became clear in the *Avant-Propos* which he wrote in 1958 to his *Actuelles III*, his selection of articles he had written on Algeria from 1939 onwards, he would almost certainly have disapproved. 'If you want Algeria to be separated from France,' he declared, 'both communities will, in a certain way, perish.'[17] To the end of his life, he thought that his father was of Alsatian descent, the son of one of the French families which had chosen, in 1870, to move from Alsace to Algeria rather than live under German rule when Alsace and Lorraine were ceded to Prussia after the defeat of France in the Franco-Prussian war. Camus was wrong in underestimating the length of time his family had lived in Algeria, and where they came from in France. His father's family had been there since the 1840s; and they were originally from Bordeaux. His mother's family had also been in Algeria for over fifty years before Camus was born. They originally came from the Balearic Isles. There was no sense, in Camus's view, in which anywhere other than Algeria could be seen as his family's home. Neither did he accept the view that his relatives could be seen as colonialist profiteers. They did not, as Camus remembered from his childhood, enjoy any higher a standard of living than the members of the French working class in metropolitan France.

They did, of course, do much better than the nine million or so Arabs living in the same country; and this was something which Camus could, with some justice, say he had tried to do something about. But the Algerian war understandably dominated Camus's life from 1954 onwards, and contributed to the artistic sterility from which he then felt he was beginning to suffer. For when you read what Camus wrote and said in the last years of his life, you get the impression of a profoundly unhappy man. Never, as far as one can judge, did he sit back in his book-lined study at the Editions Gallimard, at the heart of literary Paris, think of the magnificent house he had bought at Lourmarin, in the South of France, with the money from the Nobel Prize, remember his childhood in the rue de Lyon, and say the French equivalent of 'By golly, I made it.' It is true that his second marriage, in 1940, to Francine Faure, had not always been a happy one. His twin children, Catherine and Jean, were born in 1945, but Camus did not enjoy domestic life. He was something of a womaniser, and in 1955 went to live in a bachelor flat. In 1953, his wife had a nervous breakdown. Not all his good looks and charm of manner prevented Camus from following the pattern whereby great creative writers tend to make their nearest and dearest rather unhappy.

From 1951 onwards, Camus also became increasingly involved in the public quarrels which are so marked a feature of French literary life. Part of the interest which his books aroused in the France of 1945 stemmed from an intriguing contrast: on the one hand, there was Camus the political journalist of *Combat*, writing in terms of obvious sincerity about justice, freedom and truth; and, on the other, there was the Camus of *L'Etranger*, *Le Mythe de Sisyphe*, *Caligula* and *Le Malentendu*, for whom the world was totally absurd. Camus had already, in 1943, begun to put the two sides of his personality together in his *Lettres à un ami allemand* (*Letters to a German Friend*), and the process was virtually completed in 1945 with the publication of a short essay entitled *La Remarque sur la révolte* (*Remark on Revolt*). In it, Camus defended the existence of certain moral values, and especially that of individual human rights, and a number of ideas which the essay contained recur in *La Peste*. But when, in November 1951, Camus developed the political implications of his concept of revolt in the 286 pages of *L'Homme révolté*, the attacks on him from the left, and especially from Jean-Paul Sartre and his allies, were vigorous to the point of being quite vicious. Camus was accused of selling out to the middle classes, of abandoning all the fervour and moral purity of his early work, and of depriving the French working class, by his attack on Marxism, of all hope of improving their position.

Camus replied with some acerbity, but did not enjoy this kind of literary in-fighting. His sense of disappointment and disillusionment inspired a good deal of *La Chute*, in 1956. The unexpected award of the Nobel Prize in 1957 – everyone, including Camus himself, said it should have gone to André Malraux – attracted even more attacks. Like André Gide, Arthur Koestler, George Orwell, Ignazio Silone, Richard Wright, André Malraux and Stephen Spender, Camus was one of the many writers in the thirties and forties who began as men of the left, but who then made what those who were still sympathetic to the Soviet Union regarded as the great betrayal. He became, that is to say, a determined opponent of Soviet Communism, and even something of a cold-war warrior. Because of the size and influence of the French Communist Party in the France of the 1950s, Camus's position seemed more unusual than it would have done in an English-speaking country, and attracted more attention.

There was, at the time, no viable left-wing organisation in France to offer an alternative to the Communist Party. Camus's praise in *L'Homme révolté* for the achievements of the Scandinavian democracies, like his preference for what he called 'un travaillisme français' (a French version of the British Labour Party) received few favourable comments.

One of the few things which Camus knew about his father was an incident told to him by his mother. One day, Lucien Camus decided to take advantage of the arrangement, which did not disappear from French law until 1940, whereby the public could be admitted to the execution of criminals by the guillotine. But instead of the satisfaction which he expected to feel at the sight of a man being justly punished for an abominable crime, all he could do for the rest of the day was lie on his bed and vomit. The story recurs as one of Meursault's memories of his dead father in *L'Etranger*, and Camus tells it again in his own name at the beginning of the long essay, *Réflexions sur la guillotine*, which he published in 1957, in a joint volume with Arthur Koestler's *Reflections on Hanging*.

In addition to the now familiar objections to the death penalty on the grounds of its inherent cruelty, the lack of evidence for any deterrent effect and the irreparable danger of executing the wrong man, *Réflexions sur la guillotine* also emphasises the excessive power which this type of punishment gives to governments in their treatment of real or supposed political dissidents.

> During the last thirty years [wrote Camus in 1957], State crimes [les crimes d'Etat] have been infinitely more numerous than crimes committed by individuals ... The number of people killed by the State has assumed astronomic proportions, and is infinitely greater than that of private murders. There are fewer and fewer people condemned to death for ordinary crimes and more and more for political offences.[18]

Camus's main preoccupation as a political thinker was with the use of the death penalty as an instrument of state policy. This is one of the central themes in *La Peste*, as it had been in the articles in *Ni victimes ni bourreaux*. When, in 1981, one of the first actions of the newly elected socialist government in France was to abolish the death penalty, Camus won his greatest posthumous victory.

2

Technique, Codes and Ambiguity

Camus never actually used the term 'roman' (novel) to describe any of his books. *L'Etranger*, like *La Chute*, is a 'récit', a long short story or a *novella*. *La Peste* is 'une chronique', a chronicle, *L'Exil et le royaume* is a collection of 'nouvelles', short stories. It may be, had Camus lived to complete the book *Le Premier Homme* (*The First Man*), on which he was working at the time of his death, that he would have called it a novel. But he died before *Le Premier Homme*, which was apparently to describe the life of his father as he grew up in Algeria in the late nineteenth century, had become more than a series of preliminary drafts. The central character, someone even more culturally deprived than Lucien Camus had been in that he can 'neither read nor write, [and] has neither morality nor religion', consequently was going to be somebody who discovered the essential truths about human existence from zero. What sounds like an attempt to cast Lucien Camus in an almost mythical role would, had it been completed, have strengthened the possibility of reading Camus's work as inspired, at least at the unconscious level, by the image of his absent father.[19]

In his reluctance to use the word 'roman', Camus was following the example of a writer whom he much admired, André Gide. Out of his various prose fictions, Gide gave the title of novel only to *Les Faux-Monnayeurs* (*The Coiners*, 1926), a complex narrative that links together a large number of different characters. Like *L'Etranger* and *La Chute*, the Gidean *récit* concentrates on one issue and one group of characters. Camus's two *récits* tell an even more simplified anecdote than *L'Immoraliste* or *La Porte étroite*. In *L'Etranger*, we are told very little about anyone apart from the central character of Meursault. In *La Chute* we do not even know the name of anyone other than the narrator, Jean-Baptiste Clamence. The issues raised in *L'Etranger* are highly complex, but the story told is a direct and simple one. Meursault goes to his mother's funeral, takes Marie Cardona as his mistress, becomes involved in the affairs of his somewhat dishonest neighbour, Raymond Sintès, shoots an Arab, is tried for murder and sentenced to death. Although *La Chute* describes a large number of minor incidents, the basic story can also be summarised very quickly: Jean-Baptiste Clamence tells how he discovered that his apparent devotion to other people's interests hid an all-consuming egotism, and how he reacted to this discovery.

La Peste, though more like a conventional novel in its time sequence and characterisation, lives up to its subtitle by chronicling the arrival of the plague in the North African city of Oran in a style reminiscent at times of a reporter describing an actual epidemic. It describes how a number of individuals react to the outbreak of the disease, analyses how it dominates the lives of the whole population, and ends with the warning that, one day, the plague might 'wake up its rats again and send them to die in the streets of a happy city'. The emphasis is on the collective nature of the experience and on the depersonalising effect both of the physical plague and the spirit of totalitarianism which it represents. If you go to Camus's novels looking for a French equivalent to one of the great traditions of American or English fiction, you will be disappointed. They do not deal with the ironies and complexities of human relationships as they develop over time, and the main characters are almost always men. Even in *La Peste*, where we are occasionally invited to compare individuals with one another, only the journalist Rambert and the priest Paneloux give any sign of becoming different people as a result of what happens to them.

There are nevertheless a number of good reasons for talking about *L'Etranger*, *La Peste* and *La Chute* as novels, and for looking at the short stories in *L'Exil et le royaume* as a series of exercises in narrative technique which enable the reader to enjoy the experience which the novel has most frequently and most effectively offered: that of stepping temporarily into other people's lives. Camus's fiction tells stories, presents characters and depicts places. We are interested in what happens to Meursault, and intrigued by the kind of person that Clamence has become. We are horrified by what happens to people who catch the plague or whose lives are altered by it. We are given, in *L'Etranger* and *La Peste*, a Lawrentian-type exploration of the spirit of place, of the sights and sounds of French North Africa. In *La Chute*, we are made to feel the very different atmosphere of a rain-soaked and fog-bound Amsterdam. We may not always be as spellbound by the question of what happens next as we are when we read Balzac, Galsworthy, Thackeray or Somerset Maugham. But the moral and intellectual issues are as intriguing as they are in the novels of Tolstoy, Dostoevsky, Aldous Huxley, Graham Greene or Evelyn Waugh. Indeed, the success of Camus's novels, with their presentation of a whole range of religious, political, moral and social issues, proves that Huxley was wrong in making Philip Quarles, in *Point Counter Point*, say that the 'chief defect of the novel of ideas is that you must write about people with ideas to express – which excludes all but about .01 per cent of the human race'.[20] *L'Etranger* has sold almost five million copies. *La Peste* is well over the four million mark, while *La Chute*, a more difficult novel, has sold almost a million and a half.[21]

L'Etranger, *La Peste* and *La Chute* also fit in with some of Camus's own ideas about what a novel should be. In July 1943, he published in a review called *Confluences* an article entitled 'L'intelligence et l'échafaud' ('Intelligence and the scaffold').[22] In it, he argued that what characterised the French novel was first and foremost a constant attention to the matter in hand. French writers eschewed irrelevancies. Their works contained, he implied, none of the disgressions and moralising of a Dickens, none of the essays on the nature of history or on the ambitions of Freemasonry which hold up the action in Tolstoy's *War and Peace* or *Anna Karenina*. There is, maintains Camus, a kind of 'passionate monotony' in the way that Madame de La Fayette, Benjamin Constant, Choderlos de Laclos, Stendhal and even Proust bring everything back to the single idea which dominates the novel they happen to be writing. Eight years later, in *L'Homme révolté*, Camus expanded and developed the nature of art set out in 'Intelligence and the scaffold'. The aim of the imaginative writer, he argued, was to bring experience entirely under control, and he illustrated this idea by quoting Van Gogh's remark that we 'must not judge God by this world. It is one of his less well finished sketches'.[23] Part of what Camus means by revolt is the desire to re-create the world in accordance with the human ideas of balance, harmony and form. Although the books he published may not have the range and complexity of experience which the ideal novel satisfying the criteria outlined in *L'Homme révolté* would presumably possess, they are impeccably written and constructed.

In 1943, Camus made an entry in his *Carnets*, his working notebooks, which shows how conscious he was of problems of form. 'What attracts many people to the novel', he wrote, 'is that it is apparently a *genre* which has no style. In fact it demands the most difficult style, the one which subordinates itself completely to its subject.'[24] He then continued: 'one can thus imagine an author writing each of his novels in a different style', and this is exactly what he did. The sharp, isolated, individual notations of immediate items of physical experience which characterise Meursault's perception of the world in *L'Etranger* give way to a style which reflects the interminable, soul-destroying anonymity of the plague. This, in turn, is replaced by the self-conscious exploitation of language and by the highly complex sentences of Jean-Baptiste Clamence, a man whose style of speech reflects a mind entirely absorbed in its own problems and ambitions.

These variations of pace and spin do not prevent you from seeing the same mind in action and the same attitude to experience at work. After 1940, Camus never went back to Algeria for more than a few weeks at a time. The theme of exile plays an important role in *La Peste* and *La Chute* before becoming one of the two poles around which the six stories in *L'Exil et le royaume* are organised. In order to protect himself from the need to write books because he needed the money, Camus worked from 1943 onwards as an administrator and series editor at the publishing house of Gallimard. Many French writers take a job of this kind, and most of them can bear with equanimity the fact that it requires them to live in Paris. This created more of a problem for Camus, and the feeling of exile is also reflected in a remark in his *Carnets* for 1950. 'Yes, I do have a country. The French language.'[25] Yet, while the total mastery of this language in a number of contrasting registers is another obvious feature linking his different books together, it does not limit the ways in which they can be read.

In another of his early comments in the *Carnets*, Camus wrote that anyone who was going to set out to write novels ought to learn to think in images, and he repeated the idea in one of the first literary articles he published in *Alger Républicain*, a review on 20 October 1938 of Sartre's *La Nausée*. 'A novel', he then wrote, 'is never anything but a philosophy put into images. And, in a good novel, the whole of the philosophy has passed into the images.'[26] Each of Camus's own novels is based upon an image which it continually recreates in the reader's mind. In *L'Etranger*, it is one of a young man standing on a sundrenched beach, firing five shots into the body of an Arab, but being sentenced to death not for the murder he has committed but because he did not weep at his mother's funeral. In *La Peste*, the image is of 'a deserted town, white with dust, saturated with the smell of the sea, sonorous with the cry of the wind', which 'groans like an unhappy island' under the relentless wind of the plague.[27] If you close your eyes and think of *La Chute*, you will see a man sitting in a bar in a rain-soaked seaport, weaving an elaborate web of half-truths and perspicacious lies in order to trap his listener into the belief that all men are victims of the same self-seeking duplicity.

But the images which these books create in the reader's mind have a quality which is lacking in the ones which we find if we turn our gaze within ourselves. They do not, that is to say, suffer from the essential poverty which, in Sartre's view, distinguishes the images in our mind from the objects which we actually see in the external world. On the contrary, each is almost like the grain of mustard seed of the Scriptures, which grows from minute beginnings until it becomes a tree in whose branches all the birds of the air and all the critics of the literary world can come and lodge. Each of Camus's books can, in the language of contemporary criticism, be read according to a very large number of different codes.

This is especially true of *L'Etranger*, to which one might also apply a remark which Sartre made about William Faulkner's *Sartoris*: that good novels, with the passage of time, become 'just like natural phenomena'.[28] Like a natural object, *L'Etranger* seems to be inexhaustible in the different ways in which it can be analysed. For when it was first published, in June 1942, it was seen as a depressing example of a rather pessimistic type of realism. André Rousseaux, the well-known Catholic critic, went so far as to interpret it in *Le Figaro Littéraire* for 17 July 1942 as a study of the moral decadence of France which the new Vichy régime, with its 'Révolution Nationale' and slogan of 'Travail, Famille, Patrie', was trying to remedy. The central character of *L'Etranger*, he wrote, was a man 'without humanity, without human value, and even, in spite of the ambition to be realistic which provides the sole framework to the book, without any kind of human truth', and other critics took a similar line. J. M. A. Paratoud, writing in *Confluences* in October 1942, spoke of the 'tasteless existence' of the central character, Meursault, a man whom he described as 'lacking both will and passion'. The review in the influential *Nouvelle Revue Française* for October 1942 saw *L'Etranger* primarily as a novel of social revolt, aimed at denouncing a society which had prevented Meursault from looking after his mother properly and had thus virtually compelled him to place her in the nursing home where she died. Even after the appearance of *Le Mythe de Sisyphe*, in October 1942, had offered a more complex and positive code in which *L'Etranger* could be read, critics still tended to see Meursault as a dim, rather unsatisfactory character, the French equivalent of Erskine Caldwell's *Poor Fool*, or of the less intelligent of Hemingway's heroes. Wyndham Lewis, for example, wrote in 1952 that 'A moron is not the same as a dumb ox, but they are of the same family.' Nathan A. Scott described Meursault, in a study published as late as 1962, as a 'forlorn, dispirited *isolato* who seeks with his own indifference to match the indifference of the world'.[29]

It is certainly possible to read *L'Etranger* in this way, especially if you have not looked at *Le Mythe de Sisyphe* and at *Noces*, and are therefore not able to follow out the implications of Camus's remark that there are some writers whose books form a whole, 'in which each is to be understood in relation to the others, and in which they are all interdependent'. Indeed, there are some aspects of Meursault's attitude and behaviour which justify going even further and following Aimé Patri's example, in *L'Arche* for 1944, of thinking of him as a schizophrenic.[30] For what characterises Meursault throughout the first part of the novel is what is popularly seen as a characteristically schizophrenic tendency: he is obsessed with trivial minutiae while remaining totally indifferent to matters which most other people would regard as being of considerable importance. The book begins with the sentence 'Aujourd'hui, maman est morte' (Today, mother died), but this news seems to cause Meursault no grief. He merely comments that the message could, depending on when the telegram was sent, mean that she died yesterday.

Meursault borrows a black tie and a black armband from a friend, and sets off for the funeral. In the long-distance bus taking him to the small village of Marengo, some 80 kilometres from Algiers, he is conscious only of the smell and of the heat, and soon falls asleep. For the whole of the book, sleep plays what seems a disproportionately large part in his life, almost as though he did not want to know what was happening. He falls asleep during the night-long vigil which custom requires him to keep over his mother's coffin, is delighted to get back to Algiers after the funeral because this is going to enable him to sleep for twelve hours, and rarely seems to want to do anything at all until he has slept so much that he can't sleep any more. On the actual day of the funeral, he is conscious only of purely physical details. He notes the shining new screws sunk deep into the walnut-stained coffin, the bright colours of the nurse's clothes, the different shades of black on the hearse, on the tar melting with heat on the road, and on the mourners' clothes. He notices the blood-red earth thrown on to his mother's coffin and the white roots mixed in with it. But the only effect which these sights have on him is to tire his eyes and make him want to lose consciousness as soon as possible. While it is happening, experience is totally absorbing, and leaves no room for reflection and analysis. But once it is over, it is best forgotten.

This same apparent indifference to normal human emotions continues almost to the very end of the novel. Meursault is quite intelligent, and proves himself a very competent clerk at the shipping house where he works. His employer offers him the choice of being promoted and going to work in Paris, but Meursault declines. He is, he says, quite happy here in Algiers. But he would, he observes on another occasion, be very grateful if a new hand towel could be placed in the washroom in the afternoon. At lunchtime, when the towel is dry and crisp, it is very pleasant to wipe one's hands on it. But in the evening, when the towel has been used all day, it is damp and unpleasant. He shows no affection for his girlfriend, Marie, and refuses to say that he loves her. But he is quite happy to fall in with her suggestion that they should get married, and always notices the colour of the dresses she wears. Even when, as a result of his involvement with his neighbour, Raymond Sintès, he finds himself standing on a beach facing a group of Arabs who are threatening them with a knife, he never comments on the danger. But he does note that the toes of the Arab on the left are set very far apart.

Raymond is said to be a pimp, and although this accusation is never proved, a certain amount of what happens in the novel suggests it is true. He suspects one of his girls, an Arab woman, of cheating him over money, and wants to punish her. He persuades

Meursault to write a letter that will make the girl come and visit him so that he can humiliate her and beat her up. Meursault agrees, and Raymond carries out his plan. In spite of the girl's screams, and of Marie's presence, Meursault makes no attempt to interfere. He even goes to the police station to give evidence for the allegation that the girl has been cheating Raymond. When one of the girl's brothers, accompanied by two friends, follows Meursault, Marie, Raymond and another of Raymond's friends to the beach, Meursault first of all acts very intelligently. When the inevitable confrontation takes place, and Raymond asks whether he should shoot the Arab, Meursault dissuades him.

> But without taking his eyes off his adversary, Raymond asked me, 'Shall I let him have it?' I thought if I said no he'd get himself worked up and be bound to shoot. I simply told him, 'He hasn't said anything to you yet. It'd be unfair to shoot just like that.' Again there was the sound of water and the flute amidst the silence and the heat. Then Raymond said, 'I'll insult him then, and when he answers back, I'll let him have it.' I answered, 'All right. But if he doesn't draw his knife, you can't shoot.' Raymond started getting a bit worked up. The other Arab was still playing and both of them were watching Raymond's every movement. 'No,' I said to Raymond, 'take him on hand to hand and give me your gun. If the other one intervenes, or if he draws his knife, I'll let him have it.'[31]

It is nevertheless the presence of this revolver in his pocket which is Meursault's undoing. In order to escape from all the talk which follows the fight that does eventually take place between the Arabs and the Europeans, he goes for a walk on the beach. There, he meets one of the Arabs sitting alone near a stream. The Arab takes out the knife which he has earlier used to slash Raymond's face, and the blade glints in the sunlight. Perhaps because he is under the illusion that he is being attacked, perhaps because he can no longer stand the blazing sun and the stifling heat, Meursault clenches his hand round the revolver. The trigger gives way, and the Arab falls. Meursault then fires four more shots which are like 'four sharp blows on the door of unhappiness'.

At the trial, the evidence of his unfeeling nature provided by his behaviour at his mother's funeral tells heavily against him. So, too, do the details of his involvement with Raymond, and he is sentenced to death. On the night before his execution, the prison chaplain comes to visit him, and to offer the consolation of an eternal life beyond the grave. For the first time in the novel, Meursault is stung into saying what he really thinks. He seizes the priest by his cassock, and shouts out his belief that only the sensations of the world matter, and that in this world the inevitability of death makes everything else meaningless. Then, as the warders intervene to pull the priest away, Meursault is once again left alone with his thoughts. For the first time, he feels himself opening out to 'the tender indifference of the world', and longs, so that 'everything may be fulfilled', that there will be a crowd of spectators on the morning of his execution, and that they will greet him with cries of hatred.

For the reader coming to *L'Etranger* for the first time, the overwhelming impression is one of irony and waste. In his relationship with Raymond Sintès, the only one studied in any detail in the book, Meursault behaves as if he lacked the opposable thumb. He shoots an Arab against whom he has no personal grudge, and is then executed for a crime that arranges matters very conveniently for Raymond, a man who has pretended to be his friend only for what he can get out of him. Meursault makes no use at all of the intelligence which enables him elsewhere in the novel to comment very shrewdly on other people's behaviour, and which has made so good an impression at work that he is offered promotion. In spite of the fact that he is facing an Arab armed with a knife, and had earlier seen this knife used on Raymond, he makes no attempt to plead self-defence. At the end of the novel, he gives the impression of a man who discovers the immense importance and value of life on the very evening before he is about to lose it. When a man knows he is to be hanged in a fortnight, observed Dr Johnson, it concentrates his mind wonderfully. It is a great pity, and it seems very much Meursault's own fault, that this concentration comes too late.

In French, the image immediately brought to mind by the title of Camus's first book of essays, *L'Envers et l'endroit*, is that of a piece of cloth, which can be looked at from the right side or the wrong side. Those critics who interpreted *L'Etranger* as an example of rather ironic realism, the twentieth-century equivalent of the Maupassant short story *La Parure*, were in a sense looking at the events from the wrong side of the cloth. For Meursault is not really a brother-in-law to the unfortunate Loiselier couple, who spend their whole lives scraping together enough money to pay back the price of a valuable necklace only to discover that the jewels in the one that they lost were mere paste. There is also what you might call the right side of the cloth, a reading of Meursault's experiences which led the English critic H. A. Mason to describe him, in a review in *Scrutiny*, as 'the worthy representative of a valid attitude towards life'. Cyril Connolly, in his preface to the first English translation of *L'Etranger*, in 1946, also saw Meursault as a positive character, a man representing many of the virtues – as well as some of the defects – of a pagan attitude to life. This way of looking at the *récit* recurs in one of the most interesting books on any aspect of Camus's work, Robert Champigny's *Sur un héros païen* (*On a Pagan Hero*).[32]

Thus Meursault, as you become increasingly aware when you look at him from this point of view, is perfectly at home in the physical world and perfectly at ease in his own company. It is only occasionally that he illustrates the other meaning which the title *L'Etranger* has in French and is a stranger to himself. He gets on well with the other people in his immediate circle, who value his company and appreciate the fact that he doesn't talk very much. He has none of the nostalgia for the higher, spiritual values which makes Christians so unhappy with things as they are. Being able to sleep a lot, with what Meursault specifically describes as 'un sommeil léger et sans rêves' (a light, dreamless sleep), is not necessarily a symptom of a desire to escape from reality. It is a sign that you enjoy an enviable peace of mind. It is also, in a hot country like Algeria, a very useful accomplishment. It enables you to enjoy what Meursault likes doing: swimming, lying in the sun, making love to Marie. The absence of grief at his mother's funeral can also, in this respect, be seen as reflecting the eminently sensible pagan view that 'we owe God a death'. Meursault's mother was quite old. It was therefore perfectly natural that she should die. The Christian ritual of mourning the dead is also peculiarly out of place in a hot Mediterranean country like Algeria, where Christianity has never been more than a covering for the basically pagan attitudes which match the climate and the landscape. If Meursault declines the opportunity of working in Paris, and prefers to concentrate on the pleasant crispness of a hand towel at midday, this is because he gives justifiable precedence to the certainties of immediate physical sensations over the more dubious satisfactions offered by the bitch goddess, success. If he declines to tell his mistress that he loves her, and prefers to note, when the window has been left open while they make love, that 'it was good to feel the summer night flowing over our brown bodies',[33] this is because he prefers the realities of sensual pleasure to the conventions of romantic fiction.

It is certainly possible, even if you have never read another word by Camus, to interpret the character of Meursault in this very much more favourable and positive way. But it is even easier if you look at what Camus said about his hero, and at the links between *L'Etranger* and Camus's other books. As his *Carnets* show, Camus was disappointed at the initial reception of *L'Etranger*. He even drafted a long letter to André Rousseaux in which he drew attention to the careless way in which his novel had been read. He was consequently quite keen, once he had become better known, to take up the French custom whereby authors give extensive interviews to explain what their books mean. It was important, he told Gaëtan Picon in one of these interviews in August 1946, to take full account of 'la présence physique et l'expérience charnelle' (physical presence and bodily experience) which he saw as the essence of Meursault's character. 'The men in Algeria', he added, 'live like my hero, in an absolutely simple manner. Naturally, you can understand Meursault, but an Algerian will understand him more easily and more deeply.'[34]

This was not an idea which came to Camus only out of reaction against the negative portrait of Meursault in the first published reviews of *L'Etranger*. The *récit* is full of echoes from the very self-consciously pagan world of *L'Envers et l'endroit* and of *Noces*. Indeed, in his refusal to consider the possibility of a life beyond the grave, Meursault expresses exactly the same attitude as Camus himself. 'What was the point in being alive in my soul', Camus wrote in one of the essays in *L'Envers et l'endroit*, in 1938, 'without eyes to see Vicenza, without hands to touch the grapes of Vicenza, without flesh to feel the night's caress on the road between Monte Bercio and the villa Valmararia?' The correctness of Robert Champigny's analysis was also reinforced by a later entry in Camus's *Carnets*:

Calypso offers Ulysses the choice between immortality and the land of his fathers. He rejects immortality. That is the whole meaning of the Odyssey.[35]

The Meursault of *L'Etranger* is very much the young Camus, and the terror he feels in his prison cell is the expression of what the Camus of *Noces* calls 'this harsh confrontation with death, this physical terror of the animal that loves the sun'. He is the Camus who feels totally at home in his native Algeria, and who is like the happy barbarians celebrated in the closing essay, 'Summer in Algiers', in *Noces*. For he too loves in Algiers 'what everybody lives off: the sea visible from every corner, a certain weight of sunlight, the beauty of the race'.[36] Indeed, part of the continuing popularity of *L'Etranger*, as a novel, is in the restrained but lyrical portrayal which it gives of the delights and values to be found on the sundrenched beaches of the Mediterranean world.

In this respect, as John Weightman observed in *The Solar Revolution*, Camus is one of the authors who contributed to a fundamental change in our present attitude towards the natural world. Until the early to middle years of the twentieth century, as Professor Weightman pointed out, it was extremely unusual in any European country for people to expose their bodies to the sunlight. Camus expressed the same idea when he wrote in one of the essays in *Noces*:

> For the first time in two thousand years, the body has been shown naked on the beaches. For twenty centuries, men have tried to impose decency on the unabashed simplicity of the Greeks, to reduce the role of the flesh and to complicate our clothes. Today, reaching back over this history, the young men sprinting on the Mediterranean beaches rediscover the magnificent gestures of the athletes of Delos.[37]

One could, of course, play down the impact of this rather rhetorical sentence by pointing out that it is all simply the result of everyone having more money and paid holidays. You are given a month off work and you have to go somewhere. But just as bare mountains and gothic architecture became fashionable in the late eighteenth and early nineteenth century partly as a result of the way Rousseau, Wordsworth and Chateaubriand wrote about them, and it became fashionable to go to Scotland only after the publication of the novels of Sir Walter Scott, so the extraordinary success of the Club Méditerranée can be linked to the impact of three writers: André Gide, D. H. Lawrence and Albert Camus. All three of them, by what is perhaps more than a coincidence,

suffered at one time in their life from tuberculosis. Camus's *Noces* –
like Gide's *Les Nourritures terrestres* and *L'Immoraliste* – is very much
a book which evokes the euphoria of convalescence. Gide's works,
in what is again perhaps more than a coincidence, also describe
the same landscape as well as the same beaches and the same
scenery as *L'Etranger* and *Noces*.

It is true that Camus, while admiring Gide as an artist, did not
care for the way he 'exalted the body'. He found it too
intellectualised.[38] Camus's own paganism has indeed done more
than Gide's rather self-conscious and slightly guilt-ridden
approach to heighten the popularity of a movement which also
has its literary origins in the writings of Colette and which reached
its more vulgarised apotheosis in the Saint-Tropez of the 1960s
and the early films of Brigitte Bardot. It has made Camus, for his
readers outside as well as inside France, an almost exemplary
figure. In the 1950s and 1960s, on the beaches of Australia,
New Zealand and Southern California, a sun-obsessed mini-
culture grew up whose attitudes and ethos were often quite
extraordinarily similar to the value system underlying certain
aspects of *L'Etranger*. It was a value system which Camus had
made explicit in *Noces* before casting it into a more intellectualised
form in *Le Mythe de Sisyphe*, and whose presence in *L'Etranger* has
perhaps done more than anything else to make it so very popular a
novel.

For it could be argued, bearing in mind Rousseau's *La Nouvelle
Héloïse* as well as Camus's *L'Etranger*, Margaret Mitchell's *Gone
with the Wind* as well as the James Bond novels of Ian Fleming, that
works of fiction never become bestsellers for purely literary
reasons. They do so because they correspond, in a way that the
author himself may not wholly understand and may not have
initially intended, to a particular set of attitudes, to a hitherto
unformulated nostalgia, or to a previously unfocused desire to live
in a special kind of dream world. In the case of *L'Etranger*, the
values that Meursault is made to represent also go beyond a
purely physical preoccupation with the sunlight and with the
delights of swimming. Meursault does not say very much. In a
way which, curiously enough, corresponds to an Anglo-Saxon
rather than to a Mediterranean ideal, he is a quiet man who keeps
himself to himself. This makes him popular among his fellow
European Algerians, and one of Camus's own favourite
characters, the small restaurant-keeper Céleste, comes forward at

his trial to give evidence on his behalf and say that 'he is a man'. When asked by the lawyers to say precisely what this involves, he replies that 'everyone knows what that means'. The lawyers who represent middle-class society may not understand what he means, but for the reader of *Noces*, the reference is obvious:

> And I believe that virtue is a meaningless word throughout the whole of Algeria. Not that these men lack principles. They have their code of morality, which is very well defined. You 'don't let your mother down'. You see to it that your wife is respected in the street. You show consideration to pregnant women. You don't attack an enemy two to one, because 'that's dirty'. If anyone fails to observe these elementary rules, 'He's not a man' and that's all there is to it. This seems to me just and strong.[39]

But even if Céleste could find the words to express the importance of this rather macho ideal, the implication of the second part of *L'Etranger* is that he would not be understood. One of the obvious ways in which *L'Etranger* corresponds to Camus's ideal of relevance as the defining characteristic of French fiction is that everything in it, from the point of view of formal construction, fits perfectly together. Every incident which Meursault experiences in innocence during the first part of the book is re-interpreted in the second part as overwhelming evidence of his guilt. This gives an extra meaning to Camus's image of 'l'envers et l'endroit', the right and wrong side of the cloth, and to the dualistic sensibility which recurs in the themes as well as in the titles of his books. It also fits in with the suspicion of lawyers and of the formal processes of law which occurs as a leitmotiv through the whole of his imaginary world, and which explains why Céleste would not have been understood even if he had been able to express himself. Like Meursault, and like the Marie who breaks down in court when her affair with Meursault is evoked in formal legal terminology and says that it was 'not like that, not like that at all', Céleste is being temporarily obliged to live in what the Camus of *L'Etranger* presents as the unauthentic world of official legal proceedings and established bourgeois society. When Meursault listens to the speeches made about him by the defence and prosecuting lawyers, he suddenly hears the little trumpet of the ice-cream sellers in the upper part of the town of Algiers. He is then, as he says, assailed by memories of a life which is no longer

his, but in which he had found his simplest and most lasting
treasures: 'the smells of summer, the part of town that I loved, the
sky on certain evenings, Marie's dresses and the way she
laughed'.[40] The passage, especially when listened to in the
recording of Camus himself reading it, is an essential one for the
understanding both of *L'Etranger* and of the appeal made by
Camus's early work.

In the France of the 1940s, his celebration of the apparently
trivial sensations of ordinary life corresponded to a need made
peculiarly intense by the immediate historical circumstances of
the French people. After years spent reassuring its citizens that
there would be no war, the French government had declared war
on Germany in September 1939. It had done so, theoretically, in
order to fulfil its treaty obligations to defend Poland. Poland had
been overrun by Germany in a fortnight. Soviet Russia, until 23
August 1939 the sworn enemy of fascist Germany and the home of
the socialist ideal, had then suddenly become Germany's ally.
Less than a month later, it had joined with her in the destruction
of Poland. After having been reassured, by posters on every wall,
that they would win because they were stronger, the French had
then seen their army defeated in under two months. The Third
Republic, the régime which had made France a democratic
country and won the Great War, was declared overnight to have
been one long mistake. On 10 July 1940 it was replaced, by a vote
of 569 to 80 in a National Assembly whose members had originally
been elected in 1936 to bring in the left-wing reforms of the
Popular Front, by the very right-wing Vichy régime of 'L'Etat
Français'. The republican slogan of 'Liberté, Egalité, Fraternité'
was replaced by 'Travail, Famille, Patrie'. The French were
invited to think much of their duties and little of their rights. They
were, in addition, told that the defeat of their army was all their
fault. The greatest soldier of France, Marshal Pétain, the man
who had defeated the Germans in 1916 at Verdun, publicly shook
hands with Hitler at Montoire and urged his fellow countrymen to
collaborate with the German army which had providentially
invaded their country. In the circumstances, there was perhaps a
case for putting whatever faith you might have had left in the
apparently minor pleasures offered by the cries of ice-cream
sellers or by the pleasant crispness of a hand towel at midday.

With somewhat less political justification, the hippies and
beautiful people of the sixties and seventies responded to the

Meursault of *L'Etranger* in very much the same way. He, like them, was in their eyes an outsider in modern society because modern society was dishonest and hypocritical. Having not read any of his other works, the middle-class rebels of the 1960s even adopted Camus himself as one of their heroes. Meursault's refusal to communicate with a morally corrupt society corresponded to their own cult of neo-existentialist authenticity. His taciturnity also appealed to the still remarkably widespread view among the not-so-young as well as the young that anyone who pronounces more than two articulate sentences must be a phoney. In January 1955, this way of looking at *L'Etranger* was encouraged by Camus himself. In a preface to an American schools edition, he went much further than he had done in 1946 when trying to correct what he saw as the erroneous first readings of *L'Etranger*. Meursault, he now stated, was 'the only Christ we deserve'. He was, he wrote,

> not a piece of social wreckage, but a man who is naked and poor, in love with the sun that leaves no shadows. Far from being empty of all feelings, he is inspired by a passion for the absolute and for truth.

L'Etranger can therefore, Camus concluded, be read as 'the story of a man who, with no heroics, accepts to die for the truth'.[41]

It is certainly possible to read *L'Etranger* in this way. Such an approach does, as will be seen when it is analysed in more detail later in this chapter, have drawbacks as well as advantages, just as you need to be careful when placing *L'Etranger* side by side with *Le Mythe de Sisyphe*. For it is also equally possible, by emphasising some aspects of the text rather than others, to read *L'Etranger* in a philosophical code, as a story illustrating certain aspects of the concept of the absurd which Camus set out in his first philosophical essay. *Le Mythe de Sisyphe*, described in a subtitle as an 'essay on the absurd', was published only a few months after *L'Etranger*, in October 1942, and Camus had written them together. In both books, as the text makes clear, the idea that life has no meaning is linked to the idea of the inevitability of death. As Camus put it in 1938 in his review of Sartre's *La Nausée*, 'why this fever for life in these legs that are going to rot?' The conversation between Meursault and his employer makes it clear that his refusal to go to Paris is based on more than an instinctive

preference for a town in which, as in Algiers, people's hands and
faces are bronzed by the sun. 'When I was a student', Meursault
comments, 'I had lots of ambitions of that kind. But when I had to
give up my studies, I realised that none of this really mattered.'[42]
It is almost an autobiographical reference to the moment when
Camus was told that he was going to die of tuberculosis, and both
Meursault and his creator, the author of *Le Mythe de Sisyphe*, are
haunted by an equal awareness of the inevitability of death.

There are naturally many ways in which *L'Etranger* and *Le
Mythe de Sisyphe* are very different. Nothing could be more unlike
Meursault's apparently lackadaisical approach to life than the
attempt at rigid logical analysis which characterises Camus's
essay on the absurd. This opens with the question of whether,
since life has no meaning, we should commit suicide. In order to
answer such a question, Camus says, you have to decide what you
mean when you say that life is absurd. Such an idea is produced,
he argues, by a clash between two realities: man's desire to
explain everything in rational terms; and the fact that the world is
opaque, mysterious and irrational. But, argues Camus, if we are
to remain faithful to our experience of the absurd, if we are to treat
it, as Descartes did his *cogito*, as the one certainty in an otherwise
shifting world, then we must not abolish either of the two opposing
terms which originally brought it into being. We must not kill
ourselves, for this would take away man's desire for rational
explanation. And more importantly, we should not follow the
example of the other thinkers who have set out from an absurdist
viewpoint and committed what Camus calls philosophical
suicide.

These include Husserl, Kafka, Kierkegaard, Dostoevsky and
Jaspers, and it is an interesting reflection on the cultural life of
Algiers in the 1930s that Camus should have read so many
thinkers who were only just coming to be known in metropolitan
France. There is a reference in one of the early *Carnets* to
borrowing books from the public library, and Camus's first
publisher, Charlot, also had a bookshop. In the 1930s, Camus
owned a dog which he called Kierkegaard.[43] In his review of
L'Etranger and *Le Mythe de Sisyphe*, in 1943, Sartre made a rather
snide remark about Camus not quite understanding some of the
philosophical texts he discussed.[44] It is true that he does show
something of the enthusiasm of the autodidact in insisting that he
has read all the most up-to-date books, and you could say the

same, if you felt in an unkind mood, about *L'Homme révolté*. But you would, if you did, be missing the important point that Camus is right. The thinkers he discusses in *Le Mythe de Sisyphe*, and especially the Christian existentialist Kierkegaard, do see the concept and experience of the absurd as a kind of springboard into religious faith. They are committing what he calls philosophical suicide.

Instead of trying to escape from the absurd, says Camus, we should try to live with it, and there is a phrase in *Le Mythe de Sisyphe* which was specifically intended to be read as a commentary on *L'Etranger*: 'A temporary employee at the Post Office is the equal of a conqueror if they both have the same awareness of their own fate.'[45] Meursault, in Camus's own view, has gone through the experience of the absurd before the action of the novel begins, and has quite consciously thought through his own value system. As his outburst to the prison chaplain makes clear, he is a man who has very deliberately not made the leap into religious faith, who has not committed philosophical suicide. As he lies in his prison cell, wondering what has happened to his appeal to have the death sentence commuted to one of life imprisonment, Meursault occasionally allows himself the luxury of imagining that it has been granted. The problem then, he writes, is to

> control that burning rush of blood which would make my eyes smart and my whole body delirious with joy,

and his reaction can be read in one of two ways. As Robert Champigny argues, it is an example of the application of Stoic, pagan wisdom. In an otherwise impossible situation, Meursault derives the maximum profit from his appeal, just as he profits from the sight of the clouds he can see through his cell window. But Meursault's wild leap of joy also echoes the remark in *Le Mythe de Sisyphe* that 'the only obstacle, the only deficiency to be made good, is constituted by premature death'. In a world from which other meanings have disappeared, the only possible aim can be to experience as many conscious physical sensations as you can. In order to do this, you have to live as long as possible, and what Meursault wants to do is spend another thirty years enjoying life in Algiers. In *Le Mythe de Sisyphe*, the delight one finds in the apparently minor pleasures which occupy Meursault's attention will be made more intense by the constant awareness of our

inevitable death. This awareness destroys all other values, and
Camus sums up the whole argument of his essay when he writes
that 'la vie sera d'autant mieux vécue qu'elle n'aura pas de sens'
(life will be all the better lived in that it is meaningless).[46] Imagine
yourself in a jet aeroplane, going nowhere in particular, and
suddenly being told by the pilot that you are going to crash in an
hour or so's time. If you can so master your physical terror as still
to appreciate the unique quality which your scotch on the rocks
then suddenly acquires, you have understood one of the codes in
which *Le Mythe de Sisyphe* invites you to read *L'Etranger*.

It is true, perhaps fortunately, that there is for most of the time
no such direct, one-to-one relationship between *Le Mythe de Sisyphe*
and *L'Etranger*. The way that Meursault drifts amiably through
life is at the furthest possible extreme from the 'passion to exhaust
everything which is given' which Camus regards as characterising
the ideal heroes of the absurd. When Meursault has a free day, he
spends it aimlessly pottering about his apartment. He eats his
fried eggs without bread because he cannot be bothered to go out
and buy any. His one intellectual action is to cut out an
advertisement for Kruschen salts and stick it in an exercise book
where he puts things that amuse him. Although he may have been
a student, there is no evidence of his ever reading a book.
Meursault's awareness of death and his virtual obsession with
physical sensations nevertheless make him a kind of photographic
negative of the more vigorous heroes of the absurd celebrated in *Le
Mythe de Sisyphe*, just as his passion for truth shows itself very
clearly in the way he rejects religion. The *juge d'instruction*, the
examining magistrate responsible for interviewing him after his
crime, makes every attempt to persuade Meursault to
acknowledge his guilt and express remorse. He even implies –
perhaps correctly – that a readiness to think of what he has done in
Christian terms could make the court adopt a relatively lenient
view. But Meursault refuses. He is his own man, and will have no
truck with lies and hypocrisy. One of the main reasons why the
world is absurd is that there is no God, and there is no point in
pretending that there is.

Another of the many other codes according to which one can
read *L'Etranger* is the formalistic one. It is the first French novel to
be written without using the normal narrative tense, the *passé
simple*. The predominant tense in *L'Etranger* is the *passé composé*
('j'ai vu', 'je me suis promené', 'il a ajouté'), and the traditional

distinction in French used to be that one used the *passé simple* ('je vis', 'je me promenai', 'il ajouta') in any formal narrative, while keeping the *passé composé* either for speaking or for recording verbatim what somebody said. For a variety of reasons, this distinction is beinning to break down in contemporary French, but in 1942, when *L'Etranger* was published, it was strong enough for the impact of this particular aspect of the novel to be very considerable. Indeed, if you were to adopt the purely formalistic stance of Alain Robbe-Grillet and the other theoreticians of what used, in the 1950s, to be known as 'le nouveau roman', you could even say that the only really important fact about *L'Etranger* was Camus's decision to write his story using only the present, the imperfect and the *passé composé*. Such an approach could be highly illuminating if somewhat limiting. It would, in particular, prevent you from looking closely at what Camus meant when he said in 1946 that one of his aims had been to 'décrire un homme sans conscience apparente', to 'describe a man apparently unaware of what was happening'.[47]

As John Cruickshank pointed out in his *Albert Camus and the Literature of Revolt*, the normal convention of the French *récit*, as of the French novel in general, has always been to present the reader with a character who understood what was happening and who explained to the reader, often at some length, precisely what this was. This is certainly what happens in Benjamin Constant's *Adolphe*, as well as in Proust's *A la recherche du temps perdu* and Gide's *L'Immoraliste*, and it is indeed possible to imagine a novel in which the arguments and examples of *Le Mythe de Sisyphe* are set out in the same rational and analytical manner as the rather different view of the absurd is presented in Sartre's *La Nausée*. For obvious aesthetic reasons, Camus did not want to do this, and in the context of the immediate reception of *L'Etranger* his choice of an apparently totally unreflective hero had a supplementary if accidental advantage. Between the mid-1930s and the early 1950s, there was a great vogue in France for the American novel, and especially for the works of more violent and hard-boiled practitioners such as William Faulkner, Ernest Hemingway, John Dos Passos, John Steinbeck and Erskine Caldwell. *L'Etranger* derived some benefit from this vogue, in that it could be read as an American-style novel with a distinctively French flavour. The acuity with which Meursault noted down what he saw and felt made him sound like a Hemingway describing 'sand so white it hurt your eyes'. It was in reply to a question about a possible American influence on his work that Camus said that he used what he later described as a behaviourist approach because this suited his intention of describing 'un homme sans conscience apparente', a man without apparent awareness.

It would certainly have been difficult for Camus to combine this essentially aesthetic ambition with the depiction of a hero who did represent the world view set out in *Le Mythe de Sisyphe*. What characterises the 'absurd men' celebrated in the novel – the Don Juan, the actor, the conqueror and the artist – is the unremitting and total awareness that they have of themselves and the world. This is not an easily detectable aspect of Meursault's personality. It is even possible, as John Cruickshank also suggested, that *L'Etranger* suffers as a work of art because of the large number of apparently incompatible aims which Camus was pursuing, from a 'complicated attempt to appear uncomplicated' which led him to try to be Hemingway and Heidegger, Franz Kafka and Paul Valéry, all in the space of one short novel.[48] This is fair comment, though there is something to be said for apparently simple novels which – like *L'Etranger* – can be read in a large number of different ways. But this is far from being the most serious criticism of *L'Etranger*. Yet another code in which it can be read is that of an unconscious exercise in intellectual inconsistency.

Bestsellers tend to attract readers for non-literary reasons as well as for their literary quality. They are also sometimes like really popular chocolates in that they have a slightly soft centre. In the case of *L'Etranger*, you don't need to bite very hard to find it. All you have to do is look a little more carefully at the implications of Camus's remarks in his 1955 preface about Meursault being 'the only Christ whom we deserve' and a man who 'with no heroics, accepts to die for the truth'. It is true that Meursault does, in the second half of the novel, have so strict a regard for truth as far as his own feelings are concerned that he virtually sentences himself to death. Time and time again, in his interviews with the *juge d'instruction*, in his session with his defence lawyer and during his actual trial, he is given the opportunity of putting on an act which will ensure, if not his acquittal, at least a fairly lenient sentence for manslaughter with mitigating circumstances. A few well-chosen tears about his poor dead mother; a readiness to agree with the suggestion that he had, on the day of her funeral, put on a show of insensibility only because he had 'dominated his natural feelings'; a not too discreet reminder that he was still, on the day he shot the Arab, under the deep emotional shock of his mother's death; a sincerely phrased insistence on the terrible remorse he felt for his sin; and all would have been well. From the way Camus tells the story, you can almost see the court cheering. If he had been prepared to play the game that society expected of him, Meursault would not have needed a Rumpole to get him off.[49]

As it is, however, Meursault sticks rigidly to describing the way he actually felt. This effectively cuts the ground from under his lawyer's feet, though one is a little surprised at the lawyer's own failure to plead self-defence. Meursault was, after all, facing an Arab who was holding the very knife used only an hour or two earlier to wound Raymond. But the code in which Camus is intending this aspect of *L'Etranger* to be read is that of the novel of social protest. He is concerned, as in so many of his other works, to attack the death penalty, and his criticism is aimed here at the way in which criminal courts reach their verdicts. Instead of concentrating on the facts of the case, they introduce the kind of ir-relevant and circumstantial evidence which justifies Camus's own description of *L'Etranger* as the story of a man who is sentenced to death not for shooting another man but for not having wept at his mother's funeral. Meursault notes how his defence counsel 'didn't seem to have nearly as much talent as the prosecutor'. One of the most frequent criticisms of the death penalty is that it is wrong for a man's life to depend upon a contest of skill between two lawyers. As when Meursault lies in his prison cell awaiting execution, the description of his sheer animal terror transforms *L'Etranger* from a study of paganism or of the absurd into a socially committed novel directed against the death penalty:

> The most difficult part was that in-between time when I knew they usually operated. Once it was past midnight, I'd be waiting, listening. Never before had my ears picked up so many noises or detected such tiny sounds. I must say though that in a way I was lucky throughout that period in that I never once heard footsteps. Mother often used to say that you're never altogether unhappy. And lying there in my prison when the sky turned red and a new day slid into my cell, I'd agree with her. Because I could just as easily have heard footsteps and my heart could have burst. For even though the faintest rustle would

send me flying to the door and even though, with my ear pressed to the wood, I'd wait there frantically until I could hear my own breathing and be terrified to find it so hoarse, like a dog's death-rattle, my heart wouldn't burst after all and I'd have gained another twenty-four hours.[50]

Passages like this took on particular meaning in the late forties and early fifties, especially after Camus had become known, as a result of the publication of *La Peste* in 1947, as a determined opponent of capital punishment. He encouraged this reading by making two references to *L'Etranger* in *La Peste*, in the second of which Tarrou describes a man accused of murder as looking, as he stood in the dock, like 'an owl frightened by too bright a light'. On a number of occasions in *L'Etranger*, and especially at the moment when he kills the Arab, we are told about Meursault's sensitivity to bright lights, so that there is no danger of the attentive reader of Camus's first published novel failing to pick up the reference to him in the second. But there is a wide difference between a man sentenced to death, as Meursault is, because he has committed a specific crime recognised as such in all legal systems, and the innumerable victims of legalised but quite arbitrary state violence that Camus is talking about in *La Peste*. This difference becomes even more noticeable if you follow up the implications of the 1955 preface and look at Meursault's attitude to truth in the first part of the novel as well as in the second.

Meursault first becomes involved in the events which lead to his own and the Arab's death when he agrees to write a letter to Raymond's Arab girlfriend. This letter would inevitably have included a fair number of lies, since Raymond's intention, which he explains to Meursault, is to persuade the girl that he is still fond of her so that she will be tempted back to see him. He will then make love to her, spit in her face at the moment of climax, and throw her out. When this happens, and Raymond also beats the girl up, Meursault behaves with his customary indifference. When Marie, who is there with him, is so upset by what happens that she cannot eat her lunch, Meursault eats most of the meal himself and shows no more sympathy for her than he had done for the Arab girl. As Cyril Connolly remarked in his preface to the English translation, 'the new paganism is no kinder to women than the old', and it is difficult to square this concept of Meursault's behaviour with the way Our Lord behaved towards the woman taken in adultery in John 8:3–11. If he is, as Camus says in his 1955 preface, 'the only Christ whom we deserve', then we have fallen very low. When the police intervene and decide to check up on Raymond, Meursault again shows an attitude towards truth which is decidedly cavalier. Although he has absolutely no evidence that Raymond is telling the truth, he goes down to the police station to support Raymond's claim that the girl had been cheating him. It is not the action of a man who is 'inspired by a passion . . . for the absolute and for truth'.

None of these inconsistencies in Meursault's character would matter if Camus had not yielded to the temptation to tell his readers how they ought to interpret *L'Etranger*. There is no need, just because a novel is told in the first person, for the reader to identify wholly with the narrator or to accept either him or his values as the only ones available. Had Camus not given the 1946 interview, and even more, if he had not written the 1955 preface, the inconsistencies which make up the soft centre of *L'Etranger* would not have been so easy to detect. We should have seen Meursault, as the title invites us to do, as someone who is an outsider. He is different from us, his moral frame of reference is not the same. We should therefore take him as someone who is perhaps inconsistent, but whose inconsistencies form an integral and inevitable part of his character. We have all sometimes felt, as Meursault did in the first part of the novel, that truth was too important a commodity to be used on every occasion, and then found ourselves adopting a much more rigorous attitude when the issues seemed more important.

In the very first section of the novel, for example, Meursault has a sensitivity to other people's hypocrisy which will recur in his later refusal to do any more than describe how he thought and felt both at his mother's funeral and when he shot the Arab. When he arrives at the old people's home after the news of his mother's death, he wants to see her body straight away. But he has to wait to meet the warden, and it is only after the warden has told him a lie that he stops the caretaker from opening the coffin. Meursault knows that his mother, without being an atheist, 'had never given a thought to religion in her life'. Although he remains in character in not making his reasons explicit, it is perfectly clear to the reader that it is mainly through intellectual honesty that he refuses an active role in the religious ceremonies which take place in the first part of the novel. He wants nothing to do with a society which will not accept that some people are not interested in religion, and whose representatives tell such blatant lies.

It is only when Camus asks us to admire Meursault for a consistency in his moral attitudes which he does not in fact possess that problems arise, and from this point of view the 1955 preface to *L'Etranger* is a perfect illustration of why the approach to literature which Wimsatt and Beardsley call 'the intentional fallacy' is indeed a fallacy.[51] For the danger of paying attention to what the author says he meant, instead of solely to the text itself, is that it almost invariably ignores the complexity and ambiguity of any genuine work of art. In the case of *L'Etranger*, the comments which Camus made in 1955 have two other very noticeable disadvantages: they reflect what he thought then rather than any ideas which he might have had in mind when writing the novel some eighteen years previously; they encourage the softer minded of his readers in their admiration of Meursault as the victim both of his own integrity and of the wickedness of an insensitive and hypocritical society.

It is quite possible, in this respect, that part of the immense success of *L'Etranger* is based on the way it seems to endorse a rather facile rejection of any society with a complex legal system or an elaborate apparatus for putting people on trial for the crimes they have committed. In the 1960s, the suspicion of the state, of organised authority, and of the supposed dishonesty of middle-class society reached one of its periodic peaks in the United States, in Western Europe, and in other countries of the industrialised world. The popular enthusiasm for the sea and the sun had already begun to make Meursault an almost archetypal Mediterranean hero. The addition of the idea that he was also a scapegoat for a society of Pharisees made *L'Etranger* into a book which propagated a kind of comfortingly gloomy myth, one which said that the man of integrity was bound to be crushed by a hostile and hypocritical world. One of the more fruitful ways of approaching the argument of *Le Mythe de Sisyphe* is to see it as a more intellectualised and sophisticated version of the great principle of Protestant dissent which Bernard Shaw puts into the mouth of his Saint Joan when he makes her ask: 'What judgement can I judge by but mine own?' In the myth nourished by the soft centre of *L'Etranger*, the Protestant conscience is still there. But it has developed a number of disconcerting flaws: a readiness to admire anyone, however badly he behaves towards other people, so long as he is true to himself and makes himself unpopular with the law; the presupposition that the individual is always right and society always wrong; a lack of intellectual rigour in the endorsement of social dissent; and a readiness to accept that a wicked society will always win. They are not qualities which Luther, Calvin, Milton or Cromwell would have admired. Neither would Agrippa d'Aubigné, quoted very approvingly in Camus's *Carnets* for 1944, have had very much time for them.[52]

Camus's 1955 preface to *L'Etranger* also has another disadvantage. By inviting the reader to identify Meursault's narrative standpoint with Camus's own attitude, it makes you wonder about Camus's attitude to the Arabs who formed almost 90 per cent of the population of his native Algeria. Camus does, it is true, conclude his preface with the remark that he compared Meursault to Christ with no blasphemous intent, and solely with 'the slightly ironic affection which an artist has the right to feel towards the characters he has created'. In another of his *Carnets* he also made the rather mysterious comment that 'Toute mon œuvre est ironique' (the whole of my work is ironic).[53] While it is difficult to read *La Peste* and *L'Homme révolté* as books which say the opposite of what they apparently mean, you could read *L'Etranger* as a story which highlights the peculiarities of the person telling it. If you did this, then it would be Meursault, as a fairly typical male member of the European Algerian working class, who behaves as he does at his mother's funeral. One of the anecdotes in Herbert Lottman's biography tells how Camus and one of his friends met Sauveur Galliero, a painter whose mother had just died. Galliero told them how, on the day after the funeral, he had gone to the cinema with his girlfriend and dismissed the whole matter from his mind. Another critic, Ghani Merad, has also argued that the macho style of behaviour common among French Algerian males forbade them to cry in public, and suggested that this was a side effect of the Arab influence on them. It would certainly fit in much better with an attempt on Camus's part to depict a typical inhabitant of Algeria than with any experiment in autobiography. Camus's affection for his mother was probably the strongest emotion in his life.[54]

It would also, on this reading, be Meursault the typical North African male who does not mind arranging for an Arab woman to be beaten up. It would be Meursault, and not Camus, who describes the Arabs crouching on their heels as looking at the

Europeans 'à leur manière' (in their own special way). It would be Meursault who feels no guilt at shooting an Arab, and who provides detailed descriptions of the European visitors to his prison while relegating all the Arabs, women and men alike, to an anonymous mass. It would be Meursault who gives names to all the Europeans but who never says what any of the Arabs are called; and it would be Meursault whose killing of the Arab would be interpreted as the outward and individual sign of the genocidal instincts which are said, by critics such as Henri Kréa, to inhabit the breast of every colonising European.

As it is, however, Camus's later presentation of Meursault as a truth-telling, Christ-like figure makes the distinction between narrator and author a difficult one to sustain. It is true that the interpretation of *L'Etranger* as a racist novel appeared only in 1961, nineteen years after the novel had been published, and was inspired initially by political motives. As a European Algerian, whose ancestors had known no other country of domicile or residence, Camus had no reason to share the left-wing view that the best way to solve the Algerian problem was to send all the Europeans 'back to France'. His refusal in the 1950s to come out clearly against the use of torture by the French army contributed to his unpopularity with the anti-colonialist left, and it was two journalists writing in the left-wing *France-Observateur* who were able to put into action the wish formulated in Job 31:35 and so often granted to literary reviewers: 'Oh that mine adversary had written a book.' Henri Kréa and Pierre Nora looked at *L'Etranger* and they saw in it, as Henri Kréa rather ungenerously put it, 'the subconscious realization of the obscure and puerile dream of the "poor white" that Camus never ceased to be'.

Nine years later, in 1970, Conor Cruise O'Brien developed this particular case against Camus in a book to which he had originally intended to give the title *Albert Camus of Europe and Africa*. He found signs of an unconscious racialism in *La Peste* as well as in *L'Etranger*, and summed up his general view when he wrote:

> We may indeed accept the fact that Camus's work is a notable expression of the Western moral conscience. But we should not ignore the fact that it also registers the hesitations and limitations of that conscience and that one of the great limitations lies along the cultural frontier, in the colony.[55]

It is strange that nobody should have made quite this kind of criticism before 1961. The Tunisian-born writer Alfred Memmi had, it is true, in an article published in 1957, at the time of the Nobel Prize, described Camus as 'le colonisateur de bonne volonté' (the well-intentioned coloniser).[56] Camus's remark about preferring his mother to justice had also attracted some unfavourable comments. But by 1961, nine books and innumerable articles had been published about Camus's work. Not one of them had suggested that *L'Etranger* might be interpreted as a novel whose whole construction and pre-suppositions revealed a set of racialist attitudes which were all the more disturbing for being totally unconscious. For even if you do make the distinction between Meursault the narrator and Camus the author, the problem does not go away. It even recurs when you have a further look at *L'Etranger* as a book about capital punishment.

Camus, you then find yourself thinking, wanted to write a book in which a harmless but unconventional young man was sentenced to death primarily for his failure to observe the social convention of crying at his mother's funeral. But he had to acknowledge that however imperfect the workings of the legal system may be, this kind of thing does not happen very often. So he set up a plot in which something relatively unimportant happens: one in which an Arab gets shot in a brawl. He then wrote the story in such a way as to minimise the importance of such an event, and was able to do so primarily as a result of his own racialism. It would have been fairly unusual in such a situation, as Conor Cruise O'Brien observed, for a European to be sentenced to death for shooting a native. He would have to do something else, such as defying one of the more important of his own society's taboos. This is what Meursault does, and it is quite easy to agree with the supposition running through *L'Etranger* that it is cruel and ridiculous to cut a man's head off for his failure to behave properly at a funeral. But whatever one's views on capital punishment may be, it is harder to agree that Meursault should be sentenced merely to what he refers to as 'a few years' imprisonment or hard labour' for shooting a man who had done him no harm.

The limitations of the narrative viewpoint which Camus adopts become even clearer when you look at the events from the point of view of the Arabs. An Arab girl is brutally beaten up by a

European. The European police refuse to do anything about it, relying on the unsupported evidence of another European that the girl had been guilty of so serious a misdemeanour that she somehow deserved this treatment. When the girl's brother tries to avenge her, he is shot dead by the same European who supplied the evidence which had earlier helped to justify the police in their connivance with the brutal treatment of his sister. The European legal authorities then try to do everything possible to avoid applying the full rigour of the law. They are nevertheless forced to do so by the pig-headed obstinacy of the European murderer in not agreeing to conform with a particular set of social customs. Throughout the trial, no mention is made of the Arab who was killed.

However one-sided it is, this particular approach to *L'Etranger* is different from the other ways of looking at it only in degree. It is not different in kind, for all the different interpretations suggested in this chapter suffer from the same drawback. They all emphasise one aspect of *L'Etranger* to the detriment or neglect of the others.[57] For it is not enough to see *L'Etranger* only in the terms of the dualistic sensibility suggested by the image of the two sides of the cloth in the title of *L'Envers et l'endroit*. It is much more like a piece of shot silk, which shows a different colour each time you hold it up to the light, and a different one again every time you move it. The challenge which it therefore sets the literary critic is comparable to that of a philosophical problem. In philosophy, all the information you need is already present. What you have to do is analyse it until you find the right way of looking at the problem, until the fly, as Wittgenstein puts it, is able to escape from the bottle. There is nevertheless a difference. In philosophy, you may convince yourself, and you may even persuade others, that you have found a solution. With the kind of problem set by *L'Etranger*, even this comforting belief is impossible, and the intentionalist nature of perception is even more inescapable than it is in Wittgenstein's Duck/Rabbit. For you can look at this diagram in one of only two ways, making yourself see either a duck or a rabbit. With *L'Etranger*, there are innumerable ways in which you can look at the same text and still make sense of it. Every time you read it, you are carried away by the story and accept absolutely that this is what happened. That is the acid test of any novel, and *L'Etranger* never fails it. But every time you read *L'Etranger*, you also see it in a different light. That is one of the tests of great art.

There are many other ways in which you can read *L'Etranger* in addition to the ones outlined in this chapter, many other codes by which its various ambiguities can be explored. Germaine Brée, one of the best-known and best-informed of Camus's critics, sees it as a kind of Cautionary Tale about the Absurd. It warns us, she says, that 'in face of the Absurd, no man can afford passively to exist', and argues that Meursault is condemned, like Parsifal in the Grail legend, because of his refusal to ask questions.[58] In *The Unique Creation of Albert Camus*, the American critic Donald Lazere sets out what he calls a 'psychoanalytic view' and writes that

Once he has taken his punishment and paid the price of his penis and life, Meursault, happily reunited with his castrated real father as well, will be able to possess his mother guiltlessly, with the undifferentiated sexual identity and timelessness of infancy, in an eternal resurrection.[59]

One could also be more systematic in applying to *L'Etranger* the implications of Sartre's famous remark that 'the technique of a novelist always presupposes a metaphysic. The task of the critic is to bring out the latter before appreciating the former.'[60] In the opening sections of the novel, Meursault's experience of life is presented as a series of discrete, isolated events, unconnected by the normal conjunctions of grammatical causation. The way in which the story is told thus expresses the world of a man who has ceased to perceive life as meaningful. By a coincidence which Camus could not have foreseen when he wrote the novel in the late 1930s, it also reflects the historical situation of a culture which, like that of France in the early 1940s, has been deprived of its past and refused a future. Like all literary texts, *L'Etranger* can never be read 'sub specie aeternitatis'. It was only when the Algerian war made critics and readers more aware of the racial tensions inseparable from colonialist societies that anyone thought of analysing *L'Etranger* as the unconscious expression of a set of racialist attitudes. Since nobody can predict the future, it is impossible to say what meanings the readers will find in it fifty years from now.

In the letter which he wrote but did not intend to send to André Rousseaux, in 1942, in order to protest against his misinterpretation of *L'Etranger*, Camus wrote that it was perhaps 'a lot of fuss over a small book by an unknown writer'. From 1942 onwards, Camus ceased to be unknown, but *L'Etranger* is still not a long book. It contains less than 40 000 words, 10 000 fewer than this study of Camus's novels. Its ability to provoke so many different interpretations, and arouse so much controversy, shows that Camus established himself, with this book, as a member of that group of French novelists whom he most admired: those whose works constantly bring the reader back to the same issues. Although it can be read primarily as an exercise in narrative technique, it is also a book about values. Camus insisted on this when he wrote in his 1955 preface that it was concerned with 'the truth of what we are and what we feel . . . without which no conquest of ourselves or of the world will ever be possible'. The publication of *La Peste*, in 1947, showed a different approach to this particular problem. It had been preceded, in 1945, by the first draft for *L'Homme révolté, La Remarque sur la révolte*. This fairly short essay, which marked Camus's formal abandonment of the absurdist views running through *L'Etranger*, *Le Mythe de Sisyphe*, *Le Malentendu* and *Caligula*, also contained a series of statements which suggests a possible way of approaching *La Peste*:

> In the experience of the absurd, tragedy is an individual event. From the moment that the movement of revolt takes place, this tragedy becomes aware of its collective nature. It is an adventure in which everybody is involved. The first step forward for a mind possessed with the idea of the strangeness of the world [le premier progrès d'un esprit saisi d'étrangeté] lies in the recognition that it shares this strangeness with all other men and that human reality, as a whole, suffers from this distance from itself and from the world. The evil which, up to then, had been experienced by one man becomes a plague affecting everyone [une peste collective].[61]

3
Evil, Allegory and Revolt

There are several ways in which *La Peste* carries on the themes and atmosphere of *L'Etranger*. It is set in Algeria, in the coastal city of Oran, presented by Camus in one of his essays, *Le Minotaure ou la halte d'Oran* (*The Minotaur or the Halt at Oran*, 1940), as the commercial and sporting rival of Algiers.[62] The natural world also plays a very similar and equally ambivalent role. In *L'Etranger*, it is the sun, sea and wind, the objects of Meursault's enthusiasm, which are presented as making him shoot the Arab. In *La Peste*, the sun and wind are most frequently depicted as helping the spread of the plague. It is nevertheless by diving into the most natural element of all, the sea, that Rieux and Tarrou wash themselves temporarily clean of the stains of the epidemic. There is the same suspicion of the law, of lawyers and of legal procedures, and a statement on different terms of the rejection of Christianity which helps to give so dramatic an ending to *L'Etranger*. As the phrase in *La Remarque sur la révolte* suggests, it is also a novel about the absurd.

L'Etranger was not the first twentiety-century French novel to give particular importance to the idea that the world has no meaning. In 1927, André Malraux's first novel, *Les Conquérants*, had presented in its hero Garine a man who regarded society not as wicked or capable of improvement but simply as absurd.[63] In 1938, Sartre had commented in *La Nausée* in some detail on the particular meaning which he gave to the word in his early writings. If there is a God, he argued, the world is not absurd. He made it, and if you accept what the Bible tells you as true, He made it for man. Everything in it has a purpose, and the first chapter of *Genesis* tells us that this is a good one. But if you don't believe in God, argues Sartre, then there is no reason for anything to exist at all. There could well be nothing; and what there is could be totally different. The world is therefore, in Sartre's view,

45

absurd in the sense of having no ultimate reason for its existence. We may, through science, be able to understand the how. We shall never be able to understand the why.

Such an idea is not likely to cause much surprise to anyone who has thought even superficially about the aims and methods of the natural sciences or who has considered the philosophical implications of Darwin's *On the Origin of Species*. When asked if his researches had taught him anything about the nature of the Almighty, Darwin replied that He seemed to have an inordinate fondness for beetles. This is fair comment on the tendency of human beings to think of God as a larger and more powerful version of themselves. It is also a remark which brings out the similarities between Darwinian theory of evolution and Sartre's concept of the essentially arbitrary nature of existence. The evolutionary process has produced a million and a half different species of beetle. It has also produced Mozart. It could well have done neither; or have given birth to something entirely different.

In 1946, in the optimistic high noon of logical positivism and linguistic analysis, A. J. Ayer pointed out that there was really little justification for the distress which Sartre so obviously felt at the realisation that the world might be quite different from what it is. A world which fulfilled the demands put forward in *La Nausée* and in *L'Etre et le néant* (*Being and Nothingness*, 1943), he argued, would be even odder than the one which makes Sartre and his heroes feel physically sick at the sight of all the burgeoning and plethoric excess which characterises plants, animals and men. For it would be a world in which matters of fact were logically necessary. It would be one in which everything which existed was as completely explicable by first principles as a circle is explicable by the rotation of a straight line round a fixed point. It would be strange to live in such a world. Speculation on which horse was going to win the 3.30 at Cheltenham would be completely impossible. So, too, would all forms of human relationship.

Ayer made a similar set of comments on the way Camus illustrated his concept of the absurd in the opening pages of *Le Mythe de Sisyphe*. He too, in Ayer's analysis, was setting up a collection of demands which could not possibly be satisfied. For what he was looking for was a world in which everything was immediately and obviously put there to reassure man that he was the centre of the universe.[64] It is even possible, if you follow out this line of approach, to make the same criticism about the great cry with which Camus's Caligula announces his discovery of the absurd: 'Men die and they are not happy.' A world in which this did not happen would be just as odd as the one in which another of Sartre's ideals was realised, and in which events followed one another with the harmony and predictability of a piece of music. When Camus writes in *Le Mythe de Sisyphe* that 'no morality and no effort are *a priori* justifiable in face of the bloodstained mathematics which order our condition', he is certainly expressing in a vivid and dramatic manner the idea that we only need to count the years separating us from our two-hundredth birthday to realise that we are going to die. But awareness of this fact has been around for some time, and plenty of people have stopped believing in God and in personal immortality without concluding – as Meursault and as Camus's Caligula do – that all human actions are meaningless.

The advantage of *La Peste*, as a novel illustrating the idea that the world is absurd, is that it is not vulnerable to this kind of analysis. When the absurdity of the world takes the form, as it does in *La Peste*, of a physical disease of non-human origin, arriving for no detectable reason in a town no different from any other, killing young and old alike with a totally random unpredictability, jokes about the Almighty's fondness for beetles seem a little out of place. Plague may spread more easily if people live in crowded, unhygienic conditions. It may originally have come to Europe as one of the 'diseases of affluence', one of the deadlier gifts carried by the traders who brought the spices which livened up medieval food. But in no sense can it be placed on the same level as syphilis, radiation sickness, AIDS, lung cancer or heart disease. It is not an illness which human beings either cause or make worse by their own unwise or immoral conduct. It can be explained, if at all, only by saying that the universe makes no sense whatsoever if you look at it in terms of human ideas of right and wrong.

Such a world may make sense scientifically. Einstein maintained that God does not play dice with the universe. The laws governing it may be perfectly rational in terms of cause and effect. Their reliability is indeed essential to the work of the applied scientist. To the microbiologist, the bacillus of the plague is no more and no less irrational than the DNA code. It is only when you bring in concepts such as right and wrong, good and bad, advantage and drawback, benefit and harm, sin and righteousness, that the problems begin. It is then very tempting to use the word 'absurd' to describe a world in which plagues exist. Like bone cancer in young children, the existence of plagues illustrates the view that man lives in a world in which nature is not only morally neutral and completely indifferent to his interests. It is also a world which can, on occasion, be quite gratuitously cruel.

As a fictional chronicle, *La Peste* works on a number of different, interrelated levels, not all of which immediately seem linked to the concept of the absurd. When it was first published, on 10 June 1947, it struck most French readers as an allegory of the defeat of May 1940 and of the four years of German occupation which had followed it. When the rats come out and die in their hundreds in the streets of Oran, nobody recognises them as the unconscious harbingers of the disaster which is about to strike. When, in January 1933, Hitler came to power in Germany and immediately began to build concentration camps, persecute the Jews, and rearm on a massive scale, few people saw the danger he represented. Genocide and torture were considered, like the plague, to be diseases which had disappeared from the modern world. When the first cases of plague occur, Dr Rieux tries to persuade the authorities in Oran to adopt stringent measures to prevent the spread of the epidemic. He succeeds only when it is too late, just as France and Great Britain had decided to rearm and to stand up to Hitler only when it was too late for the Third Republic and almost too late for British democracy to ensure their continued survival.

When, in 1940, the Germans had taken less than two months to defeat the French army, they divided France into several different zones. Alsace and Lorraine simply became part of Germany, as they had been from 1870 to 1918. The *départements du Nord* were declared a *zone interdite* (forbidden zone). The north of France, together with the whole of the Atlantic coast, was occupied by the German army. The remaining third of the country was known as *L'Etat Français*, and administered by the Vichy government. It all happened very quickly, and communication between the different zones was very difficult.

When the number of people taken ill by the plague becomes too high for the authorities in Oran to pretend that nothing is happening, a state of siege is proclaimed and a rigid quarantine immediately cuts off Oran from the outside world. There too, it all happens very quickly, and the 'sudden separation into which people who were not prepared for it are plunged' exactly mirrors the situation in which the inhabitants of Paris had been prevented almost overnight from travelling to Strasbourg, Bordeaux or Toulouse. The inhabitants of Oran can communicate only by telegram, so that their most intimate feelings have to be condensed into phrases such as 'Am well. Thinking of you. Love.'[65] The French of 1940 had been allowed by the Germans to exchange news of what was happening to them only by printed cards on which they had to underline the ready-made formulae which applied. The first of the sections in which *La Peste* describes and analyses the feelings of separation which were 'the principal suffering of this time of exile' first appeared in 1943, in a collection entitled *Domaine français*. This was published in Switzerland and circulated in France in defiance of German censorship. There was, for the French readers of 1947, no danger of the various allusions to the political ordeal they had just undergone not being recognised. When the memory of how a million and a half French soldiers spent four and a half years in German prisoner of war camps was still fresh in everybody's mind, it is not surprising that the long passages in *La Peste* analysing the experience of separation should have struck so deep a chord.

The relevance of *La Peste* to the recent historical experience of the French was also particularly well marked in another incident which takes place early in the novel, the first sermon given by Father Paneloux. From a literary point of view, this attempt to explain the arrival of the plague in terms of the readiness of the God of the Old Testament to intervene directly or indirectly in the affairs of men matches some of the other great sermons of the Western novel. In its use of rhetoric, it is on the same level as the address by Father Mapple at the beginning of Herman Melville's *Moby-Dick*. It may even reflect the direct influence on Camus of the book which he described in 1952 in his essay on Melville as 'one of the most overwhelming myths ever invented on the subject of the struggle of man against evil, depicting the irresistible logic which finally leads the just man to take up arms first against creation and the creator, then against his fellows and against himself'.[66] In its vision of the nature of God as the stern chastiser of the wicked, Paneloux's first sermon also recalls the attempt to suggest what eternity might mean when measured by human concepts of time which so terrifies Stephen Dedalus in James Joyce's *Portrait of the Artist as a Young Man*. To the connoisseur of more tolerantly

Albert Camus

observed endeavours to frighten the congregation, it is like the splendid address by Cousin Amos to the Church of the Quivering Brethren in Stella Gibbons's *Cold Comfort Farm*. In the construction of *La Peste*, it has another advantage: it brings together the first two of the various levels on which the novel works. It is the first step towards making what is an allegory of the German occupation of France into what Camus calls 'the most anti-Christian' of his books.[67]

In his first sermon, delivered to a crowded cathedral on a day of violent wind, Father Paneloux explains to the terrified inhabitants of Oran that the plague has been deliberately sent by God in order to punish and instruct them. Too long, he tells them, they have neglected God for the pleasures of this world, and wearied His patience by their evil-doing. But now, He has decided to punish them, and show them the way to salvation through suffering. This central message of Paneloux's sermon is not only inspired by the large number of passages from the Old Testament which, like Isaiah 7:20, illustrate how God shaves with a borrowed razor; it is also a fairly faithful reproduction of how the Vichy government, which took power in France after the defeat of 1940, explained to its citizens why this defeat had taken place.

This was not, whatever de Gaulle had suggested in his famous broadcast from London on 18 June, because the French army had simply been faced by an enemy which had more tanks and more aeroplanes. It was, according to the Vichy government, because the French had been very wicked in electing the left-wing Popular Front government of 1936, in going on strike, in obtaining holidays with pay for the working class, in listening to jazz, in encouraging the surrealist movement, and in reading immoral and ungodly authors such as Marcel Proust and André Gide. God, whose constant preoccupation was always with the especial salvation of the French, had therefore sent the German army to punish them. The description of the defeat of 1940 by the royalist author Charles Maurras as 'la divine surprise' (divine surprise) shows that Camus was not simply making it all up.[68] Neither was he the only imaginative writer to select this aspect of the Vichy ideology as a theme in one of his books. Jean-Paul Sartre's play *Les Mouches* (*The Flies*, 1943) shows the inhabitants of Argos being required by a recently established dictatorship to express personal and repeated remorse for the murder of their lawful king, Agamemnon, by the usurper Aegisthos. This, too, was a very clear allegory of the German occupation of France and of the official reaction to the defeat of 1940. Jean Dutourd's very amusing novel about the financial triumph of a grocer's family as a result of the black market which flourished during the Occupation, *Au bon beurre* (*The Milky Way*, 1952), also has a number of passages which read like a series of direct paraphrases of Paneloux's sermon.

In *La Peste*, however, Camus goes beyond the political commitment of *Les Mouches* and beyond the social satire of *Au bon beurre*. Paneloux's sermon is more than a reminder to his readers of the fact that certain elements in the Roman Catholic church in France did support the Vichy régime, especially in its early days, because it tried to bring the French back to God. The view of the universe which it presents is an essentially providential one. Human beings may suffer, but they do not suffer for nothing. Even though He may chastise His children, God remains their Father. The suffering He inflicts upon them is for their own good. The world is not absurd, since even happenings as apparently terrible as an outbreak of plague form part of a divine plan. Paneloux's second sermon, an equally irresistible candidate for inclusion in any 'Anthology of Sermons from Imaginative Literature', presents this plan from a very different point of view.

For between these two sermons, a child dies of the plague. The six-year-old son of Judge Othon dies in terrible agony, with Dr Rieux, who is leading the fight against the disease, standing with Father Paneloux at his bedside. After the child has died, the doctor turns to the priest with an obvious and terrible comment: 'He was innocent, and you know it', and the debate in *La Peste* moves at that point quite decisively away from political allegory and on to the level of religious and philosophical argument. From a Christian point of view, there is nothing in the death and suffering of children during wartime that cannot be reconciled with a belief in God. Even the hundreds of thousands of Jewish children murdered by the Nazis can be explained, within the framework of Christian theology, by the fact that human beings are free. God, wishing to give man the inestimable joy of choosing to worship Him freely, has granted all human beings the ability to choose between good and evil. Men may choose to do evil, as the Nazis did when they decided to kill all the Jews, and as Pierre Laval did when he let the Germans know in July 1942 that he would have no objection to their rounding up all the young Jewish children in unoccupied France as well as those who were over sixteen.[69] But this is in no way an argument against the existence of a God who, as the Christians teach, is at one and the same time all-powerful and all-good. Even the most evil of men are exercising the freedom which God has given them, and which is an indispensable part of the concept of good. Nobody who could not choose between good and evil could reasonably be described as committing a virtuous act, or could be seen as deserving salvation by either faith or works.

If, however, the suffering imposed upon children is the result of a natural disease of non-human origin, and if Christianity continues to describe God as an all-powerful and all-loving Father, then there is something of a problem. A God who was all-powerful could save the child from dying of the plague. A God who was entirely good would wish to do so. But since the child dies, and does so as the result of a natural event for which no human being is responsible, then there are only three possibilities. Either God cannot save him, in which case He is not all-powerful. Or He does not wish to save him, in which case He lacks even the most basic of human moral attributes. Or He does not exist, and we both live and die in an absurd world. Not only is it totally indifferent to man, and completely inexplicable in its impact on him; it is, at times, actively hostile to him.

In spite of his lack of religious belief, Camus did not share the anti-clericalism which was so dominant a feature of French left-wing attitudes and policies in the nineteenth and early twentieth centuries. The prison chaplain in *L'Etranger* weeps when Meursault rejects his offer of comfort and consolation, and is presented as a man who is totally sincere in his beliefs, even if misguided in holding them. In *La Peste*, Father Paneloux is an attractive character who soon loses the touch of intolerance which made his first sermon so eloquent a reflection of the exploitation by the Vichy régime of the concept of God presented in the Old Testament. In his second sermon, delivered to an emptier cathedral, Paneloux ceases to address the congregation as 'You'. He speaks of 'Us' and 'We', and does not present the death of a child as a sign of God's direct and providential intervention in the workings of the universe. He recognises that the challenge which the undeserved suffering of the innocent offers to the believer is a real one. He explicitly rejects the argument that the agony suffered by the child can be justified by the existence of a future reward in heaven under the form of a happiness so great that this merely mortal agony will seem as nothing. He insists that we cannot be certain that this will happen, and argues that no Christian, 'whose Master has known suffering in his limbs and in his soul', could possibly entertain such a doctrine. For the Paneloux of the second sermon, the only way in which a Christian could interpret in Christian terms the death in agony of an innocent child would be to see it as being somehow willed by God in order to test his own personal faith.

> Father Paneloux said that the virtue of total acceptance that he was talking about was not to be understood in the limited sense normally given to it, that it was not a matter of banal resignation or even of difficult humility. We were concerned with humiliation, but with a humiliation to which the person humiliated gave full assent. Without doubt, the suffering of a child was humiliating for the mind and for the heart. But this was why we must enter into it. But this was why, and Paneloux assured his congregation that what he was going to say was not easy to say, you had to will it because God had willed it. Only thus would the Christian avoid nothing, and with all ways of escape closed to him, carry out the essential choice in all its depth. He would choose to believe everything in order not to be reduced to denying everything.[70]

Like Paneloux's first sermon, his address after the death of Judge Othon's son is a magnificent piece of writing. In his presentation of the one character in *La Peste* who is faced with a genuine intellectual and moral dilemma, Camus places some emphasis on the fact that Paneloux is a Jesuit. One of the most important features of the training given to members of that Order is a rigorous attention to the presentation of reasoned and systematic argument. Both of Paneloux's sermons are, from that point of view, part of Camus's creation of a character who is believable within the context of a work of fiction that is realistic as well as allegorical. But although the controlled eloquence and mastery of language which characterise both Paneloux's sermons represent a considerable tribute to Camus's powers of invention, it would be a total error to see the ideas expressed in either sermon as in any way reflecting what Camus himself either thought or believed. He did not like the Vichy régime, and had been a member of the resistance movement. In addition to the entries in his *Carnets* which show how conscientiously he had noted down from the Old Testament the passages in which God had made use of plagues and pestilence to help or instruct His chosen people, he also described Christianity itself as a doctrine of injustice.[71] He develops this idea in the opening chapters of *L'Homme révolté*, a book in which he is saying what he himself thinks, and his agnosticism is very firmly based on what C. S. Lewis called 'The Problem of Pain'.

Part of his aim in writing Paneloux's second sermon was indeed to criticise a particular style of Christian thinking. 'Rieux said', he noted in his *Carnets* for 1944, 'that he was God's enemy since he was fighting against death and that it was even his job to be God's enemy.'[72] Rieux is the narrator in *La Peste*, and the principal spokesman for Camus's own ideas. In his account of Paneloux's second sermon, Camus is also presenting a set of ideas which he already criticised in *Le Mythe de Sisyphe*. These did not need much expansion or development to become, in 1951, the more sustained defence of agnosticism in the first part of *L'Homme révolté*. But the most important aspect of Paneloux's sermon does not lie in any satirical intent on Camus's part or in any active hostility towards Christianity. Its essential contribution to making *La Peste* 'the most anti-Christian' of Camus's books lies elsewhere. If this, one is tempted to say, is the only way in which Christians can maintain their beliefs when confronted by the central problem of the suffering of the innocent, then they have boxed themselves into a peculiarly indefensible philosophical corner. Camus is observing their dilemma with considerable sympathy. But he can find no more of a way out of it than they can.

When, in 1945, Camus denied that he was an existentialist,[73] he was thinking partly of what separated him from Sartre. Unlike Sartre, he believed that man was more than the sum of his acts. After the publication of *La Remarque sur la révolte*, he also differed from Sartre in believing in certain moral values such as the primacy of the individual, and the gap between the two writers became unbridgeable after the attack on communism in *L'Homme révolté* in 1951. But in 1945, Camus was thinking primarily of what separated him from the Christian existentialists whose reaction to the absurd he had already analysed and rejected in *Le Mythe de Sisyphe*. It is their ideas which Paneloux is paraphrasing and reproducing in his second sermon, and which Camus is again inviting his reader to reject. From this point of view, the difference between the two texts is one of emphasis and approach. The thinkers in *Le Mythe de Sisyphe* are depicted as mistaken. By using the concept of the absurd as a springboard into religious faith, they are being unfaithful to one of the two terms which originally produced it. They are giving up the demand for rational explanations which gave birth to the absurd when it came into conflict with the fact that the world is not a rational place. They are worshipping an absurd God precisely because He is absurd, but the debate in which they are involved is primarily concerned with the philosophical issues involved in the problem of knowledge. In *La Peste*, the leap of faith recommended by Paneloux is made necessary by the emotional and moral issues stemming from the death of a child.

The vocabulary which Camus uses in *Le Mythe de Sisyphe* nevertheless anticipates Paneloux's sermon in a way that emphasises the continuity between the two texts. Kierkegaard, writes Camus, 'gives his God three attributes of the absurd: unjust, inconsistent and incomprehensible', and Camus finds the same tendency in another existentialist thinker, the nineteenth-century Russian philosopher Leon Chestov. He, in Camus's interpretation,

> even suggests that this God is perhaps full of hate and hateful, incomprehensible and contradictory, but the more hideous his face is, the more he asserts his power. His greatness lies in his contradictory nature. The proof of his existence is his inhumanity. We must leap into him and, by this leap, free ourselves from rational illusions.[74]

The first reaction of the plain man when reading *Le Mythe de Sisyphe* is to say that Camus is making it all up. The second reaction, on discovering that the thinkers analysed in this 'Essay on the Absurd' are saying exactly the same as the seventeenth-century philosopher Blaise Pascal and the Christian theologian Tertullian, is to say that only very clever men could be so silly. For Pascal urged his readers to make a wager on God's existence which enabled them to realise that the last step which human reason made was to recognise his own impotence,[75] and Tertullian said that he believed in Christianity precisely because it was absurd (*Credo quia absurdum est*). The third reaction is to say that if you can keep believing in God only by abandoning all normal rational criteria, it might be a better idea to give up religious belief altogether.

This, indeed, is what Camus is suggesting that his readers should do. His own view is put forward by Rieux, who tells Paneloux that he will 'refuse until the moment of his death to love this creation in which children are tortured'. Rieux also tells Tarrou, in a later conversation, that 'since the order of this world is shaped by death, might it not be better for God if we did not believe in Him, and struggled with all our might against death, without lifting our eyes to the heavens where He keeps silent'.[76] This is an echo of the famous lines in Alfred de Vigny's *Le Mont des oliviers*:

> Le juste opposera le dédain à l'absence
> Et ne répondra plus que par un froid silence
> Au silence éternel de la Divinité.
> (The just man will face absence with scorn, and reply only by a cold silence to the eternal silence of God.)

It reminds us that Camus is using the novel for very much the same purpose that the nineteenth-century writers of both England and France used poetry. Although Tennyson's *In Memoriam*, unlike Arnold's *Dover Beach*, ends on a note of reconciliation, both poems deal with the same problems as *La Peste*. Both, that is, talk about human suffering in an absurd world, and the only difference is one of vocabulary. Tennyson's 'Nature, red in tooth and claw' evokes the same idea of a cruel and purposeless world as does Camus's *La Peste*. It is also a world which is just as devoid of a divine, providential plan. Arnold's 'darkling plain' where 'ignorant armies clash by night' anticipates another aspect of *La Peste*, the depiction of a world where history has no meaning. From this point of view it does not matter if the events are taking place in France in the 1940s or in the Lisbon of the 1755 earthquake. It was this manifestation of nature's indifference to man which inspired Voltaire to write *Candide*, the work in French literature which most resembles *La Peste*, and Camus's second novel is a work of philosophical argument whose theme is so universal that it could be happening anywhere. But because *La Peste* is set in Oran, and evokes the fairly specific circumstances of occupied France, the reaction to it of a number of French critics has not been one of undisguised admiration.

Sartre, it is true, greeted it in a footnote to *Qu'est-ce que la littérature?* (*What is Literature?*, 1947) as a good example of what committed literature could be. Other writers and critics have been less kind. One of the most aggressive was Jean-Jacques Brochier. Writing in 1970, ten years after Camus's death, he described him, in a short but vitriolic book, as a *Philosophe pour classes terminales* (An ideal philosopher for sixth-formers), and it is easy to see what he means. The French nineteenth-century philosopher Auguste Comte considered that the habit of metaphysical speculation was characteristic of the adolescence of mankind. After the belief in religion and magic which marked the childhood of their race, men and women moved to the stage of thinking in abstract, philosophical terms. This is very much what Camus is doing when he makes Paneloux and Rieux debate the nature of God, and it is not surprising that adolescents in the English- and French-speaking countries should have found *La Peste* almost as fascinating a book as *L'Etranger*. In one of its central preoccupations, *La Peste* exactly corresponds to the delight which teenagers take in sitting up all night over coffee arguing about God. It can even have the same effect on people who are technically adults but who have not succeeded in shaking off this aspect of their adolescence. But for disciples of August Comte, and for critics such as Jean-Jacques Brochier, the preoccupations satisfied by *La Peste* are those which genuine adults should have outgrown. Since the kind of speculation encouraged by Paneloux's two sermons in *La Peste* can give no firm answers, it should be abandoned in favour of those intellectual activities which can. These consist primarily of a more determined attempt to ensure that fewer and fewer children die as a result of the wickedness and folly which human beings display in their economic and political activities. Metaphysical speculation, such critics argue, should give way as quickly as possible to political action.[77]

This line of argument involves looking more closely at *La Peste* as an allegory of the German occupation and the resistance movement. Superficially, this allegory is quite satisfying, and there are times when *La Peste* reads better as an indirect account of the events and atmosphere of the 1940s than as a description of any actual outbreak of an infectious disease. The predominant emotion in such a situation is most likely to be an intense fear of catching the plague and a constant suspicion of your neighbour as a person likely to pass it on to you. It might well not be the anguish of separation analysed in such detail in *La Peste*. In any real epidemic, cinemas, restaurants and theatres would remain closed. If such potential centres of infection stay open in Camus's Oran, it is because the cinema was the most popular form of entertainment in occupied France, and because the French theatre enjoyed one of its many golden ages in the early 1940s. It is also because both orthodox and black-market restaurants offered a very acceptable way of supplementing the very meagre rations then available to the French. It was not only because Paneloux's first sermon reminded the French of Vichy's cult of national repentance that French readers of 1947 saw *La Peste* as an allegory of their recent political misfortunes. It was also because the teams of voluntary health workers organised by Tarrou to help Rieux reminded them of some important aspects of the resistance movement; and because they knew that Camus had been a member of the *Combat* network. The resistance was made up of volunteers who placed themselves in much greater danger of arrest and torture than ordinary people. Anyone who joined Tarrou's 'équipes sanitaires' ran a greater risk of catching the plague.

But at this point, the allegory begins to break down. There is all the difference in the world between trying to stop the spread of an impersonal disease, for which nobody is responsible and which has no identifiable aims, and trying to kill Germans. Hitler's ambitions were evil and insane. But they were identifiable: he wanted to murder all the Jews and make Germany top nation. Anyone in the resistance movement had to do more than fight the Germans. He had to try to kill other Frenchmen. The Vichy government had its own police force, *la milice*, whose aim was to defeat the resistance, and some of its members had their own idea of France which was not always entirely evil. It was at least arguable that parliamentary democracy had failed in France, and that what de Gaulle himself called 'the old Gallic propensity to quarrels and divisions' might be better held in check by a more authoritarian régime of the type which Vichy had tried to establish. In order to fight against the resistance, the Germans took hostages. A resistance fighter who killed a German officer might, by his action, cause the death of fifty or more of his fellow countrymen whom the Germans would kill by way of reprisals.

Camus's defence of *La Peste* against criticisms of this kind is contained in an open letter which he wrote to Roland Barthes in

1955.[78] It consisted largely of saying that since the people who were in the resistance movement did have to cause the death of other human beings, the representation of their struggle in *La Peste* must be an accurate one. It is not one of Camus's better prose passages. As is often the case, it is the book itself which provides the best answer to any criticisms levelled against it, especially when the nature of these criticisms is borne in mind. For in the case of *La Peste*, these criticisms were quite often politically motivated, and stressed the fact that Camus made no mention of any measures to avoid a recurrence of the plague. Any real city visited by such an outbreak would want some reassurance by the chief medical officer that the drains had been cleaned out. If, as its constant reference to the German occupation of France suggests, *La Peste* is about political evil as well as physical disease, might it not be a good idea to suggest how one might change the political system which allowed this evil to exist, particularly when this was one which had made Oran so unable to defend itself?

In the atmosphere of post-war France, these criticisms were based on a way of thinking about politics which seems less obviously true today than it did then. The most virulent form of totalitarianism, it was argued in the 1940s, was fascism. Fascism was, as Lenin had maintained, the form that capitalism took as it entered the final, deadly stage which preceded its imminent collapse. Hitler's Germany, whose domination over Western Europe is so well represented by the symbol of the plague, was the perfect illustration of how capitalism gives rise to fascism. If, therefore, we want to avoid a recurrence of fascism, the best thing to do is get rid of capitalism. This will also be a much more practical approach to the death of children than the empty protest against a non-existent God which takes up so much time in *La Peste*. As Sartre observed in his open letter to Camus in the August number of *Les Temps Modernes*, infant mortality is much higher in working-class areas than in the homes of the bourgeoisie.[79] The best way to prevent children from dying is to introduce more social justice, and such an improvement can be produced only by socialism.

In his most revolutionary period, during his editorship of *Combat*, Camus may well have thought this way himself. By the time he wrote *La Peste*, however, he had rather changed his mind. The series of articles entitled *Ni victimes ni bourreaux*, published in November 1946, show the way his thoughts were moving, and the preoccupations of these articles find their way into *La Peste* through the episode known as 'Tarrou's confession'. This episode suggests a way of reading *La Peste* which is much more fruitful than Camus's insistence on its accuracy as a portrayal of the resistance movement. It also suggests a reply to the criticism that the weakness of *La Peste* as an allegory of occupation and resistance deprives it of all value as a work of political analysis.

As in the case of *L'Etranger*, the theme of capital punishment is introduced quite late into *La Peste*. Once there, however, it colours everything which has gone before. The novel ceases to be an allegory, a work in which there is a one-to-one relationship between the story apparently being told and the events it actually depicts. It becomes a broader, symbolic work, which invites us to think about the whole phenomenon of totalitarianism, of the left as well as of the right. Initially, Tarrou is introduced as an enigmatic, rather ironically minded observer, whose description of Oran recalls Camus's own acount of the birthplace of his second wife, Francine Faure, in the essay called *Le Minotaure ou la halte d'Oran*. Like Camus, Tarrou goes into some detail about the bronze lions which decorate the front of the municipal buildings ('la mairie'), and which were still there in 1985. In his fondness for swimming and for the simple pleasures of life, Tarrou is not unlike Meursault. At times, you even think that he is the kind of man that Meursault might have grown into if he had not been afflicted with such sensitivity to sunlight and such intermittent honesty. He takes the same pleasure that Meursault does in noting the slightly peculiar behaviour of certain people. Just as Meursault describes in some detail how a little old woman once came and sat down at his table in Céleste's restaurant, ticked off the items on the menu, ate at a furious pace while still feverishly ticking the radio programmes in a magazine, so Tarrou notes with great interest the behaviour of an old man whose one pleasure in life seems to consist of luring cats to a point beneath his balcony where he can spit on them. But Tarrou soon ceases to be a figure who reminds us that Camus might, without his powerful, sometimes unconscious obsessions, and without his interest in ideas, have become a relatively minor, humorous writer specialising in the very odd way people sometimes behave. Like Camus himself, Tarrou has an obsession with capital punishment which is firmly linked to his memories of his father.

Camus's novels are not strong on family relationships. When

the examining magistrate asks Meursault if he loved his mother, he replies that he was quite fond of her ('j'aimais bien maman'), but that this didn't mean anything. All sane people, he adds, had more or less wished for the death of their loved ones, and this repetition of a remark which Camus had made in his review of Sartre's *Le Mur* in 1938 makes the magistrate's clerk hit a wrong key on the typewriter.[80] Although Rieux is married, he and his wife have no children and his wife leaves Oran before the epidemic breaks out. She is suffering from tuberculosis, and dies before the end of the plague allows them to be reunited. Rieux's mother comes to look after the house, and provides an oasis of calm as she sits and knits. But their relationship, though clearly a very affectionate one, plays only a very minor part in the novel. Clamence, for reasons which are obvious when you read *La Chute*, is not married, and none of the characters in *L'Exil et le royaume* have family relationships which form an important part of their lives.

Camus was certainly aware of the fact that the works of what he called his 'first two cycles' were not novels in the usual sense of the word but 'myths on the scale of his passion and anguish'.[81] By his own account, he had inherited from his mother's side of the family a Castilian reserve which prevented him from talking much about personal feelings. If the picture of his own childhood in *L'Envers et l'endroit* is correct, he was brought up in a family whose members did not talk about their feelings. What you have never had, you can never give, and the emotional sterility which seems to have characterised his early, crucial years did not provide that rich humus of emotional experience which has fed the imagination of so many other novelists. It is nevertheless curious, and adds weight to the view that all imaginative literature has its roots in the traumas of early childhood, that Tarrou's confession should begin with his memories of his father. The same, albeit in a different way, was true of Meursault.

In the French legal system, there is a clear separation between the lawyers who represent the state and those who assume responsibility for the interests of private individuals. The former, who are known as 'procureurs', 'avocats généraux' or 'substituts', always fulfil the same role in any criminal trial. They have the task of proving that the accused is guilty; they also have the responsibility of recommending what penalty should be imposed. Tarrou's father, a man of some eminence in his profession, has reached the rank of 'avocat général', chief public prosecutor. He is anxious that his son should follow the same career, and invites him to come and watch him in the closing stages of a trial. On doing so, however, Tarrou is so horrified by watching his father's demand for the death penalty that he leaves home. He becomes a professional revolutionary, fights on the losing, republican side in the Spanish Civil War, and remains active until one day, in Hungary, he is present at an execution by firing squad. The physical horror of what he sees, with the executioners' rifles so close to the victim's chest that they make a hole large enough to contain a man's fist, convinces him that no cause, however noble, can justify such butchery. It also inspires him to undertake a quest for a kind of innocence, and even of sainthood, which will enable him 'no longer to be a bearer of the plague'. For he has come to realise, as he tells Rieux, that 'what's natural is the microbe. All the rest – health, integrity, purity (if you like) – is the product of the human will, of a vigilance that must never falter'.[82]

Tarrou's confession does more than link *La Peste* to *L'Etranger*, and look forward to the 1957 essay, *Réflexions sur la guillotine*. It gives *La Peste* its coherence as a symbolic evocation of the two great problems of the human condition: the physical suffering of the innocent in an absurd universe; the suffering which human beings inflict upon one another. True revolt, as Camus maintained in *La Remarque sur la révolte* and argued in more detail in *L'Homme révolté*, lies in man's attempt to create the human values of justice and reason in a universe from which they are so conspicuously lacking. This is what Rieux is trying to do, and why the choice of a doctor as the narrator and central character in *La Peste* is so important. But revolt, in Camus's view, is also the driving force behind man's attempt to create social justice; and it is in the context of the problems which this ambition creates that Tarrou's confession takes on its full significance.

By 1947, Camus had become more conscious of the dangers of revolution than of its advantages. It could, as the example of the Soviet Union and its satellites went to show, make an unjust society even worse. It did so, in Camus's view, because of the tendency of the revolutionaries themselves to see problems only in abstract terms. Instead of living individuals, they saw only social classes. This led them, in the terms of Tarrou's confession, to become bearers of a particular kind of plague, what he called 'la fureur du meurtre' (the rage to kill), which showed itself in the increasingly widespread use of the death penalty for political ends.[83] Time and again, in *La Peste*, the plague is referred to as 'l'abstraction'; and there is a particular phrase in Tarrou's confession which makes it very clear what this means. Everyone, he tells Rieux, carries the plague within himself, and we all have to keep a ceaseless watch over ourselves in order to avoid, in a moment of absent-mindedness, breathing into another person's face and infecting him. We are all capable of spreading the disease of totalitarianism because we are all capable of intolerance. We all have a tendency to think in the terms of an abstract ideology rather than of real people.

It is in this respect that Tarrou's confession suggests an answer to the criticism that *La Peste* proposes no answer as to how the repetition of an evil such as Nazism can be avoided. In 1960, the Israeli secret service captured Adolf Eichmann and brought him back to Israel. He then stood trial in Jerusalem in 1961 for the part he played in the murder by the Nazis of some two million Jews. But once in the dock, this 'medium-sized, slender, middle-aged' man, with his 'receding hair, ill-fitting teeth, and nearsighted eyes', looked like a minor civil servant, the kind of man who, if you produced the right documents, would renew your road fund licence. There was absolutely no correlation between the insignificant, ordinary-looking individual, and the immense, almost unimaginable crimes of which he was guilty. 'Except for an extraordinary diligence in looking out for his personal advancement,' writes Hannah Arendt in her *Eichmann in Jerusalem: A Report on the Banality of Evil*, 'he had no personal motives at all.' The same would probably have been true of the dedicated Russian civil servants who helped Stalin, a man whose score of dead bodies, as George Steiner remarked in *The Portage to San Cristobal of A.H.*, made the Nazis seem like amateurs. There would again have been no proportion between any of these individuals, as individuals, and the terrible acts they had committed when inspired by an ideology and acting as part of an organisation.[84]

The problem of understanding the evil which such human beings represent becomes even greater if you accept that the people who gave them their orders were all trying to achieve what they thought of as the good. Even in ordering the murder of six million Jews, Hitler was not setting out to do something that he thought was wrong. He was trying to purify the German race. It was an insane ideal, but it was an ideal. The people who helped him were not all sadists. Indeed, as Hannah Arendt pointed out in her account of Eichmann's trial, 'a systematic effort was made to weed out all those who derived physical pleasure from what they did'.[85] The millions of victims sent to die in the Soviet prison camps were sacrificed in order to achieve the age-old dream of a totally just society.

When Paneloux uses his first sermon to try to justify the plague, presenting its arrival in Oran as part of God's purpose, he is falling victim to a comparable disease to the one which afflicted the followers of Hitler or Stalin. The dramatic image which he uses of the plague, that of a great flail beating down the human wheat until the grain is separated from the chaff, has the effect of blinding both him and his congregation to what is actually happening. He is, when he speaks in these terms, both the victim and the exploiter of an abstraction, just as the ideologists of Nazism were when they evoked the Aryan ideal, or the apologists of Stalin were when they justified the death of five million kulaks by the need to modernise Soviet agriculture. All the misfortunes of humanity, says Tarrou in his confession, come from the fact that men do not say clearly what they mean. George Orwell remarked in *Politics and the English Language* that it is more honest to say 'I believe in killing off your opponents when you can get good results by doing so' than to say that 'the rigours which the Russian people have been called upon to undergo have been amply justified in the sphere of concrete achievement'.[86] At least you are not fooling yourself or deceiving other people.

Not all political action, of course, involves policies which need to be formulated with such brutal frankness. When, in 1966, the second volume of Camus's *Carnets* appeared in an English translation, Philip Toynbee picked out for special comment the remark in which Camus said that he could not go in for politics because he could not bring himself to wish for the death of his adversary. 'Impossible not to think of Mr Wilson and Mr Heath *looking* daggers, no doubt, across the floor of the House', he wrote, 'but surely never tempted to use them.'[87] It was an observation which highlighted the difference between the Continental style of politics, which the events of the mid-twentieth century had taught Camus to regard as inevitable, and the political behaviour which seemed more natural to an inhabitant of the British Isles. Camus's political world, like that of Sartre, is very much the reflection of mid-twentieth-century European politics. In that world, the first thing you did when you got power was to start killing your opponents, either with or without a certain number of legal formalities. This is what *La Peste* is talking about, and in so far as politics have now begun to take a more civilised form in Western Europe, parts of Camus's novel have begun to date. The same is true of the one great English novel about totalitarianism, George Orwell's *Nineteen Eighty-Four*. But in 1947, memories in Europe of the killing plagues of right- and left-wing totalitarianism were still very acute. What Camus is describing is the way in which quite ordinary people had helped to spread this plague by what they had said and done at apparently quite unimportant moments. Standing behind and beside Eichmann in the Jerusalem courtroom were all the Germans, Austrians and Poles – and all the English and French – who had either made anti-semitic remarks themselves or failed to react when such remarks were made in their presence. When *La Peste* appeared in English translation, a critic in the *Times Literary Supplement* entitled his review 'The Plague within us'. It was a justified extrapolation of Tarrou's insistence on how difficult it is not to be a bearer of the plague. On the right, there were few in the 1930s and 1940s who had not at some time applauded the vigour of the new Nazi régime. On the left, there were perhaps even fewer who had not at some point observed, on hearing of Stalin's atrocities, that you can't make an omelette without breaking eggs.

Camus's *Carnets* for 1939 and 1940 show that he greeted the outbreak of the Second World War with a distinct lack of enthusiasm. This is perhaps why *La Peste* presents the phenomenon of totalitarianism as the twentieth-century equivalent of the 'spiritual wickedness in high places' of which St Paul speaks in Ephesians 6:12, and not as a more concrete form of evil that you can fight against by force of arms. Although Camus denied both that he personally was a pacifist and that *La Peste* was a pacifist novel,[88] Tarrou's confession argues that spiritual evil can ultimately be defeated only by spiritual means. Violence, in the short term at any rate, breeds only further violence, and the Europe of 1947 did not give much encouragement to anyone inclined to argue that the military defeat of fascism had produced a decisive and overwhelming political improvement. Half of the countries conquered by Hitler were now ruled by Stalin. The other half, France included, were threatened by the prospect of a violent revolution which could lead to only one of two things: the imposition of a form of left-wing dictatorship comparable to the ones recently established in Hungary, Poland and East Germany, and shortly to be set up in Czechoslovakia; a third world war as the Americans moved in to counter what they would see as a new example of Soviet expansion.

This was not, it is true, quite the kind of reading which Sartre had in mind when he made his complimentary reference in *Qu'est-ce que la littérature?* But it was the way that more conservatively minded critics saw *La Peste*, and how it inevitably reads nowadays when replaced in the political atmosphere of post-war France. For like *L'Etranger*, *La Peste* is also a bestseller which owes its popularity to non-literary as well as to literary reasons. It marked, in French society just as in Camus's own development, the beginning of a retreat from the enthusiasm for revolution which had been so distinctive a feature of the thirties and forties. At the same time, it suggested that this enthusiasm should be replaced by a more sober assessment of what political ideology could achieve. The modesty of this approach to the problems of society is made very clear, within the book itself, by the importance given to the character of Joseph Grand. He is not, Camus emphasises, a particularly inspiring or heroic figure. He is a tall, gangly, fifty-year-old clerk in the municipal offices in Oran, whose wife has left him and who devotes the whole of his leisure time to trying to write a novel. But since he is obsessed by making this novel begin with a sentence so perfect that everyone in the publisher's office will immediately take off his hat to salute the arrival of a masterpiece, he never makes any progress. Like Sisyphus, who was condemned to push a rock to the top of a mountain only to see it roll down again, he no sooner gets one word right than all the others look wrong. He is therefore doomed to constant repetition and failure, and sometimes seems less happy with his lot than the hero of Camus's 'Essay on the Absurd'. But Camus nevertheless presents him as the hero of the story,[89] and there is a phrase in *La Remarque sur la révolte* which explains why.

Grand makes a fairly modest contribution to the fight against the plague. He keeps a statistical record of the number of cases reported, and there is an obvious contrast between this somewhat unexciting task and the dramatic defiance of an absurd and tyrannical world by the left-wing heroes of Malraux's *La Condition humaine* and *L'Espoir*. But the action of the trade union secretary who keeps his accounts up to date, Camus writes in *La Remarque sur la révolte*, is 'metaphysical revolt, just as much as the spectacular daring which sets Byron up against God'.[90] By stubbornly persevering in an apparently thankless task one can contribute to the 'obstinate, disorderly but inevitable improvement of the human lot'.[91] In 1945, Camus saw this as the characteristic which most clearly distinguished French socialism from the Messianic and absolutist version developed by orthodox Marxists, and it is when you look at it in the context both of Tarrou's confession and of the remarks about Joseph Grand that *La Peste* does become a politically committed novel. To be against the more extreme versions of revolutionary action and ideology was, in the France of 1947, to be against the Communist Party. This was an important and quite courageous attitude to recommend at the time, and Camus won few friends when he made the underlying political ideology of *La Peste* more explicit four years later in *L'Homme révolté*. This book performed, as the Cambridge philosopher Richard Wollheim observed, 'a great service to liberal thought' by arguing the case for a non-Marxist approach to political rebellion, and a useful comparison can be made between Camus's defence of moderation in politics and Karl Popper's preference in *The Open Society and its Enemies* for the superiority of 'piecemeal social engineering' over totalitarian socialism.[92] But *L'Homme révolté* did not, in the Paris of the early 1950s, improve Camus's standing in the French intellectual and literary world. The fact that it sold 75 000 copies within a year of publication is from this point of view an instructive reflection of the discrepancy between the reputation which a book can have with those theoretically best qualified to judge it and the appeal it makes to a wider audience.

La Peste has also been criticised by left-wing thinkers for other reasons than the appeal its idealism makes to sixth-formers. They have attacked its apparent substitution of the ethic of the Red Cross – or even of the Boy Scout movement – to that of the revolutionary activist. Its North African setting, in particular, made it vulnerable to the same kind of criticisms that were levelled against *L'Etranger* after 1961, and it is clear in retrospect that Camus made something of a tactical blunder in the way he introduced the character of Rambert. Within the overall conscious structure of the novel, Rambert fulfils two fairly obvious functions. He is a visitor to Oran, and has left behind him in Paris a mistress with whom he is deeply in love. He stands, therefore, as an individual example of those thousands of separated lovers whose sufferings are analysed in *La Peste*, and whose situation, as Camus observed, was so characteristic of the 1940s. After a number of attempts to escape from Oran, Rambert eventually accepts the idea that 'no man is an island, entire of itself', decides deliberately to share the fate of the people with whom he has happened to find himself, and joins Tarrou's 'équipes sanitaires'. He thus illustrates the theme of humanist solidarity which runs through the novel, and would be quite successful as a slightly edifying minor character if it were not for the weight given in the first section of the novel to his original reason for coming to Oran. This was to report on the living conditions of the Arab population, and his first conversation with Rieux gives the impression that it is the criticism of French colonialism which is about to become one of the main themes of the novel. When Rieux asks him whether his paper will print a total condemnation of these conditions, the presupposition is that Rambert may send home a series of articles which are as devastating as Camus's *Misère de la Kabylie* had been in *L'Alger Républicain* in 1939. But the Arabs then totally disappear from the novel, to the point of not even being mentioned as falling victim to the plague. All the characters in *La Peste*, as in *L'Etranger*, have European names.

It is true that the frequency of Spanish surnames in Rieux's chronicle is a fair reflection of one aspect of the racial balance of Oran. Even today, quite a number of Spanish fishermen live and work undisturbed in that part of the Algerian Socialist Republic. But although Oran was the most Europeanised of the cities of French Algeria, the total absence of any Arabs from *La Peste* does rather lay Camus open to the same kind of criticism which it became fashionable, after 1961, to make of *L'Etranger*. He is, in other words, revealing the hollowness of his humanism by treating the Arab population merely as a convenient backdrop to a series of wholly European preoccupations. There is little to interest a Moslem in the exclusively Christian debate about the action and attributes of God developed in Tarrou's two sermons. The allegory of the German occupation of France is also pretty meaningless to a population whose experience of Europeans did not allow them to make distinctions about the various types of oppression available. Neither would the implications of Tarrou's confession have been particularly interesting to members of a culture which had not, in the 1940s, known totalitarianism from the inside. When seen in the light of Camus's declared ambition to be a Mediterranean writer, *La Peste* is a North African novel only to the extent that the highlands of Kenya used to be called white.

These criticisms are, of course, valid only if you are sufficiently removed from the common sense of the plain man not to query two of the established doctrines of twentieth-century literary criticism. The first is that you can appreciate and criticise an author for aspects of his work which he did not deliberately put there and which he perhaps did not even know existed. The second is that you can take a book out of its immediate historical context and look at it in the light of ideas which few people held when it was originally published. The disadvantage, as far as *L'Etranger* and *La Peste* are concerned, is that the application of these doctrines brings out defects rather than qualities; and this is not a result which shows literary criticism at its best. An emphasis on the real or alleged racialism of *L'Etranger* and *La Peste* also has the effect of suggesting that the Camus who wrote these two novels was somehow dishonest. Either this was conscious, in that he deliberately decided to use the Arabs merely as convenient walk-on characters to illustrate essentially European concepts. Or it was unconscious, and revealed that Camus was so imbued with the instinctive racialism which dominated the mentality of the French settler population in Algeria that the moral fervour which runs through *La Peste* is doomed to ring hollow as soon as you try to sound it out in any real situation.

La Peste is also vulnerable, as a political novel, to criticism from the right. It is certainly true that one way of fighting against totalitarianism is by thinking and speaking so clearly that you are never taken in by any ideology. When Camus writes that 'a time always comes in history when the person who dares to say that two and two make four is punished by death',[93] he is again making a very Orwellian point. One of the first victims of totalitarianism is the notion of objective truth. This is why Winston Smith, when being tortured by O'Brien in *Nineteen Eighty-Four*, also tries to insist that two and two make four. But Hitler was not stopped by people believing in objective truth. He was defeated because the Americans, British and Russians killed over two million Germans. Stalin was not prevented from taking over Western Europe by people insisting that two and two make four. He was stopped by a series of political decisions, one of them involving the immediate use of force, all of them implying a readiness to use it under certain circumstances.

The invasion of South Korea on 25 June 1950, by heavily armed troops from the Communist North, looked at the time like a probing operation, comparable in intention to Hitler's remilitarisation of the Rhineland in March 1936 or the Anschluss of March 1938. There is little reason to see it any differently nowadays. The attempt to force the Western allies out of Berlin by the blockade of 1948 also seemed at the time – and still seems now – like a move to neutralise West Germany before taking it over in the same way that Poland, Hungary and Czechoslovakia had been taken over. The Berlin airlift held the Russians off, just as President Truman's decision to send American troops to defend South Korea in 1950 discouraged comparable acts of aggression by proxy elsewhere. In 1962, after Camus's death, President Kennedy's refusal to allow the Russians to install their medium-range rockets in Cuba had a similar effect. Deprived of what he had clearly intended to use as 'a side-arm persuader', Mr Krushchev gave up the attempt which he had been making since 1958 to blackmail the Western allies into giving up West Berlin.[94]

These political comments are not irrelevant either to *La Peste* itself or to the various meanings which it had for the readers of the forties and fifties. Both Camus and his wife seem to have thought in the 1940s and early 1950s that Russia was preparing to invade Europe. Simone de Beauvoir tells of Francine Camus's declared intention of killing herself, with her two children, on the day the Russians entered Paris; and of Camus's determination to join the resistance movement against the Russians as he had done earlier against the Germans.[95] Tarrou's remark about his contemporaries being 'tous dans la fureur du meurtre' is clearly aimed at the methods by which Communism was being imposed in Eastern Europe, and when *La Peste* is replaced in the political atmosphere of the France of 1947, it is very much a cold-war novel. Nine years later, in 1956, Camus's articles in *L'Express* were encouraging his readers to be highly suspicious of Soviet Communism.[96] It was then that he warned against the temptation of believing that the leopard of totalitarianism might change its spots, and his work both in journalism and in the theatre showed that he was, in the late 1950s, a fairly vigorous cold-war warrior. In *Actuelles III*, the collection of articles about Algeria which he published in 1958, he made this very clear when he wrote:

We must consider the demand for Algerian national independence as being at least in part one of the manifestations of this new Arab imperialism of which Egypt, overestimating her strength, wishes to be the leader, and which Russia is exploiting for anti-Western strategic ends.[97]

Neither was Camus's 1959 adaptation of Dostoevsky's *The Possessed* entirely a work of pure theatre. His comments on the prophetic nature of Dostoevsky's vision gave very much the impression that he regarded the highly reactionary analysis of socialism in *The Devils* as still being very applicable to the second half of the twentieth century.[98] There is a marked continuity in the political thinking which starts with Tarrou's confession, goes through *L'Homme révolté* and culminates in the 1959 presentation of certain forms of socialism as being, quite literally, inspired by the Devil. But at no point did Camus supplement these general warnings about the nature of totalitarianism by any recognition of the specific political decisions whereby it could, in the forties or fifties, be kept out of Western Europe.

It would be too much to expect any French writer, even one so independently minded as Camus, to speak approvingly of NATO or of the Marshall Plan. Anti-Americanism was, if anything, even more widespread in French intellectual circles in the 1940s than it is today. But once you begin to think about the wider implications of Tarrou's confession, it is hard to resist the temptation to say that the Camus of *La Peste* was a man who willed the political end without being prepared to endorse the military means. Admittedly, it is hard to see how *La Peste* could have remained a work of art if Camus had used it to indicate precisely how the latest breed of rats could be kept out of the streets of London, Paris, West Berlin and Rome. One of the major disadvantages of committed literature is that the solutions it proposes are rarely convincing or specific enough to remedy the evils it denounces. But it is disappointing not to find, among Camus's many *obiter dicta*, any acknowledgement of the strong possibility that the plague of totalitarianism was kept out of Western Europe after the Second World War by the readiness of the United States to put Chicago, Des Moines and New York at risk in order to protect the inhabitants of West Berlin.

Camus's analysis of totalitarianism in *La Peste* is based upon the idea that men are basically good and are led astray only by false ideas. 'The evil which is in the world', Rieux is made to declare in a central section of the novel, 'almost always comes from ignorance, and good intentions [la bonne volonté] can do almost as much damage as wickedness [la méchanceté] if they are not enlightened.' There is, he adds, 'no true goodness or proper love without all the clearsightedness possible',[99] and the characterisation in *La Peste* reinforces this essentially optimistic view of human nature by including only one person who is not inspired by good intentions. This is the black-marketeer, Cottard, and even he acts immorally only because he has 'an ignorant, that is to say a lonely heart'.[100] The idea that tyranny is caused by people who know perfectly well what they are doing and are determined to create as much suffering as possible in order to reinforce their political power is totally absent from Camus's imagination. Such a concept again makes *La Peste* vulnerable to criticism from right-wing thinkers who share the robust belief of *La Chanson de Roland* that 'Païens ont tort et chrétiens ont droit'. It also goes against Dostoevsky's view that human beings make one another so unhappy because they are all equally infected with original sin. But it does help make Camus's second novel a splendid illustration of how right Jean-Jacques Brochier was when he called him a *Philosophe pour classes terminales*. If there is one topic more exciting for sixth-formers to discuss than the existence or non-existence of God it is the problem of whether human beings are fundamentally good or basically bad. The major drawback to the treatment of *La Peste* as a kind of intellectual assault course in political thinking for adolescent and even adult minds is that it tends to neglect Camus's insistence that he was primarily an artist.

You could say, in the nicest way, that if this aspect of his work is so often neglected by the critics, he has only himself to blame. He should not have written such interesting books. This is not a charge one can level against Alain Robbe-Grillet, Marguerite Duras or even Samuel Beckett. If their novels are appreciated for their aesthetic qualities, it is because the challenge of the ideas is less apparent than it is in *L'Etranger* and *La Peste*. It is not easy, when discussing *La Jalousie*, *Moderato Cantabile* or *Watt*, to put into practice Baudelaire's injunction that literary criticism should be personal, passionate and political.[101] When discussing *La Peste*, it is inevitable.

You might almost say, in this respect, that an approach to *La*

Peste primarily as a work of art, with the emphasis on its qualities of construction and style, runs the risk of making it seem a less interesting novel that it actually is. Such an approach would, of course, acknowledge how many of the ideas sparked off by *La Peste* stem from the fact that it is, ostensibly at any rate, a work of fiction. Had it been an analysis in essay form of the problems of the absurdity of the world, of Christian belief, and of the evil that men do to one another, it would have raised fewer echoes in the minds of its readers and opened out less exciting vistas to their imagination. The advantage of a work of art, as is shown by the example of *L'Etranger*, is that it has the inexhaustibility of a natural object or a living being. The more you look at *La Peste*, the more interesting it becomes. The same is not true of an essay, and there is a sense in which the greatest tribute that one can pay to the aesthetic quality of *La Peste* is to follow out the various trains of thought which it inspires without ever being able to exhaust them.

There are nevertheless almost as many different aspects to *La Peste* as a work of art as there are to it as a book about the problem of evil. It is, first and foremost, what D. H. Lawrence might have called an exploration of the spirit of place. Oran is presented with an ironic affection, as when Rieux's narrative or Tarrou's notebooks comment on the ugliness of the buildings or the obsession with commerce that characterises its inhabitants. There are passages which combine lyricism with a boding menace, as when the flowers arrive in all their abundance in the markets of the town, only to wither under 'the double weight of the heat and of the plague'.[102] There are the ever-present wind and sun, seemingly in alliance with the plague as they heighten the sufferings of a whole people held captive by the epidemic. It is, especially to the medically unqualified, a vivid and frightening book, with a realism in its description of the physical effects of the disease which makes you finger your own neck uneasily to see whether the glands are starting to swell up.

It is also, as can be expected from what is in many ways an historical novel, a comparably vivid evocation of a particular time. The account, with all the appropriate administrative terms, of how the events of the 1940s heightened the bureaucratic control which the state had over its citizens is brilliantly written, with just the right mixture of menace and humour. Since totalitarian régimes never look anybody up except for their own good, it is essential for the relatives of anyone who has caught the plague to go into quarantine. When Tarrou and Rambert visit one of the isolation camps, in a football stadium, the description inevitably recalls for the French reader the internment of the Parisian Jews in the Vélodrome d'hiver after they had been rounded up by the police in July 1942. But you do not need to know about this specific incident to be reminded of the innumerable camps for supposed enemies of the state and for displaced persons which disfigured Europe in the first half of the twentieth century. When the inhabitants of Oran are described as 'this stricken people of which a part was daily fed into the mouth of a furnace and disappeared into oily fumes, while the rest, in shackled impotence, waited their turn',[103] there is no mistaking the plague which sent six million Jews to the gas chambers. However much you try to see *La Peste* in the politically neutral terms suggested by Camus's desire to be seen primarily as an artist, you keep coming back to the fact that the best description of it was provided by Camus himself when he said of *L'Homme révolté* that it was 'an attempt to understand his time'.[104] If, from this point of view, certain aspects of it have dated, then we are the more fortunate.

4
Lawyers, Guilt and Satire

However different *L'Etranger*, *La Peste* and *La Chute* may be from one another in style, construction and theme, they all have one apparently minor feature in common: a strong suspicion of the formal processes of law in general and a dislike of lawyers in particular. Although the *juge d'instruction* (investigating magistrate) who interrogates Meursault after the murder of the Arab does everything he can to find mitigating circumstances for the crime, he is presented as a figure of fun who cannot really cope with Meursault's honesty. At one point, he waves a crucifix in Meursault's face, and asks him rather hysterically whether he believes in God. When Meursault says no, the *juge d'instruction* is disconcerted to the point of declaring that his own life is made meaningless by Meursault's atheism. At that point, he becomes a rather facile illustration for Camus's demonstration of the superiority which Meursault's awareness of the absurd gives him over all the official representatives of bourgeois society. Although the court seems at times to be bending over backwards to get Meursault off, Camus's presentation of its procedures is tinged with an almost Voltairean irony.[105] It is almost as though he wants the reader to think that it is more reasonable to shoot a man because the sun is shining in your eyes than it is to stick to the rules which society has developed in order to try to arrive at some semblance of justice.

The fact that Tarrou's determination to fight against capital punishment stemmed originally from the experience of seeing his father delivering a speech for the prosecution is not the only example in *La Peste* of this hostility to the legal profession. The child who dies of the plague is the son of another *juge d'instruction*, Judge Othon, a man who does not endear himself to the reader by finding the argument in Paneloux's first sermon 'absolutely irrefutable'. After the child's death, Tarrou asks the rather

75

curious question: 'But who can feel sorry for a judge?', clearly expecting the reply 'Nobody.' It is true that Camus does make some amends later on in the narrative by describing how the judge volunteers to join the 'équipes sanitaires',[106] but Tarrou's question still leaves a slightly unpleasant taste behind it. In *L'Etat de siège*, the play which took up a number of the themes in *La Peste*, the father of the young and attractive Victoria is a judge. He is a thorough hypocrite, and is fully prepared to betray Victoria's lover, Diego, to the character representing the plague since this will mean that he is acting according to the law. When his wife points out that although he may have the law on his side, she has right on hers, there is a strong echo of the suspicion of all social institutions which has characterised so many European novelists, playwrights and poets since the outbreak of Romanticism.

When the narrator in Camus's third novel, *La Chute*, first published in May 1956, speaks of his 'instinctive scorn for judges in general' and of his inability to understand how a man 'should designate himself to exercise this surprising function', one whose existence he accepts rather as he does that of grasshoppers, though without quite understanding why,[107] he gives very much the impression that this is Camus talking about himself, and making fun of his own obsessions. There is also a very conscious irony running through the book, stemming from the knowledge of the French legal system which Camus knew he could count on his French readers having. For Clamence is an *avocat*, and as such would normally be entrusted with the responsibility of ensuring that his client is either acquitted or receives a reduced sentence. It is only if his client decides to *se constituer partie civile*, to link his interests as injured party to those of the state, that a French *avocat* appears for the prosecution. An *avocat*, of course, is not the same thing as an *avocat général*, the rank held by Tarrou's father in *La Peste*. He, like the *Procureur de la République* and his *substituts*, has the task in a criminal trial of trying to prove the guilt of the accused. But in general terms the French see the *avocat* as essentially someone who is on the side of the accused, and the word has something of the same resonance which it has when we read in The First Epistle General of John, 2:1–2: 'And if any man sin, we have an advocate with the Father, Jesus Christ the righteous; and he is the propitiation for our sins.'

The irony running through *La Chute* is that although Clamence is by the very nature of his profession what Rumpole of the Bailey is by conscious choice, someone who does not prosecute, everything which he says is aimed at making his listener feel guilty. What would normally, since he is an *avocat*, be *une plaidoirie* (speech for the defence) becomes *un réquisitoire*, a speech for the prosecution, and he actually uses the word in the last of the six sections into which the *récit* is divided.[108] The ambition which inspires him, as he does his Ancient Mariner act in the Mexico City bar in Amsterdam where the unnamed listener first comes across him, is to describe himself in such a way as to show that his imperfections are those of the whole human race. When the listener eventually but temporarily leaves his company he will be, like Coleridge's wedding guest, a sadder and a wiser man.

The implication of *La Chute* is that as soon as anyone describes his defects to us in sufficient detail, we shall recognise him as a portrait of ourselves. This is what Clamence does, and Camus's technique of narration in *La Chute* is essentially that of Browning in his dramatic monologues. As in *My Last Duchess*, we are left to infer the listener's reactions from the occasional remarks which the speaker makes, and the listener in *La Chute* has another similarity with Gigadibs, the literary man, who sits uncomplainingly throughout the 850 or so lines of *Bishop Blougram's Apology* 'while the great bishop rolled him out a mind / Long crumpled, till creased consciousness lay smooth'. This listener is an intelligent member of the middle class – in fact, as we discover in the very last paragraph, an *avocat* himself. It is conceivable, and this perhaps explains why *La Chute* has been less of a runaway bestseller than *L'Etranger* or *La Peste* – 1 386 000 copies as against 4 852 000 and 4 165 000 – that only a member of the bourgeoisie would be able to appreciate what Clamence was getting at. A manual worker might well have problems in understanding what he was talking about. A successful businessman would laugh at him. An aristocrat would reprove him for his impertinence. The book has also been a less outstandingly successful illustration than *L'Etranger* and *La Peste* of Camus's appeal as a 'philosopher for sixth-formers'. The issues it explores are those which afflict the middle-aged. Clamence's problems have little spontaneous appeal for adolescents.

It was nevertheless in the year immediately following the appearance of *La Chute*, in 1957, that the Nobel Prize for literature was awarded to Camus for 'his important literary production, which with clearsighted earnestness illuminated the problems of the human conscience in our times'. Like *L'Etranger*, which contrasts an individual's notion of truth with that of the society in which he lives, or like *La Peste*, which looks at the religious and social implications of the existence of evil, *La Chute* is a book about a moral and philosophical problem. What it discusses is the attitude we should have to our own inadequacies.

It is also Camus's most obviously autobiographical book. There are, of course, traces of his own experience and situation in *L'Etranger*. Like Meursault, Camus had a spell working in a shipping office, and also seems to have been slightly less efficient than his hero – who is good enough to be offered promotion – when he worked as a clerk in the Préfecture d'Alger. On one occasion he gave the same registration number to two different cars.[109] Meursault also has the same love of swimming as Camus himself, the same appreciation of the minor pleasures of life in a Mediterranean seaport, and the same memories of a dead father. But in *L'Etranger*, Camus was not exploiting these personal details in order deliberately to create a character whom the reader would recognise as autobiographical. He was compensating for his relative lack of inventive or imaginative powers by picking out aspects of his own personal experience which fitted in with the mood and ideas he was seeking to communicate.

In *La Chute*, the situation is very different. By 1956, Camus could count on being sufficiently well known for Clamence to be immediately recognised by the average literate French reader as a detailed if critical self-portrait of Camus himself. Admittedly, since he started life as the son of an officer, Clamence is not of quite such humble social origin. Perhaps rightly, Camus resisted the temptation to satirise the edifying, slightly 'Smiles Self-Help' aspect of the way he personally had emerged from poverty through a combination of hard work and native wit. But he does make Clamence into an obviously autobiographical figure when he makes him say that the only places in which he feels innocent are the theatre and 'Sunday football matches watched by a capacity crowd'. In a letter in 1950 to the well-known critic Pierre de Boisdeffre, Camus had said that the football field was the only place in which, during his youth, he had learnt anything about morality. An appreciation among French literary men of the character-building virtues of games is sufficiently rare for the remark not to have passed unnoticed, and it was also quite widely known that Camus had, during his youth, kept goal for the Racing

Universitaire d'Alger.[110] In 1953, Camus had expressed his continuing interest in the theatre by putting on his own adaptation of Calderón's *La Devoción a la Cruz*, and of the sixteenth-century French playwright Pierre Larivey's *Les Esprits* at the Festival d'Angers. In May 1955, he gave an open-air lecture in Athens on the future of tragedy, and was already planning the 1956 production of Faulkner's *Requiem for a Nun*. In talking about Clamence's passion for the theatre, he was consequently making references which he knew that many of his readers would recognise. This was even more the case when he gave Clamence his well-known charm and ease of manner, his popularity with women, his taste for the precise and accurate use of the French language, and his capacity for being on the side of the angels in any political dispute with strongly moral overtones.

At one point, Clamence seems almost to be reading aloud from two of Camus's recently published essays. In 1952, Camus had gone back to Algeria after a long absence. It had rained, and as he walked through the streets of Algiers, he 'read his age on faces he recognised without being able to put a name to them'. He had visited the Roman ruins at Tipasa, celebrated in the sensual lyricism of *Noces*, only to find them surrounded by barbed wire. The visit had seemed to him, in the period of depression into which he was then entering, to symbolise the final loss of his youth. It was only when the sun broke through on the last day that he was able to emerge from his gloom and reassert the 'will to live without refusing anything that life offers' which was, as he said, the virtue he 'honoured most in the world'. The essay entitled *Retour à Tipasa* (*Return to Tipasa*) appeared in 1954 in the volume *L'Eté* (*Summer*). It had thus been available for two years when Clamence said in similar terms, when evoking the idyllic atmosphere of his early manhood: 'I was altogether in harmony with life, fitting into it from top to bottom without refusing anything of its ironies, its grandeur or its servitudes.'[111] Both in its content and in its phrasing, Clamence's remark was so similar to what Camus had published under his own name that the resemblance was a positive invitation to identify the author with his fictional character.

As its title indicates, and as is emphasised by the New Testament reminiscences of its narrator's name, *La Chute* is full of Christian symbolism. It is also a book which deals more fully than any other of Camus's works with the commandments of

Christianity, and Clamence's description of his behaviour in this respect reads like a deliberate echo of a passage from another essay in *L'Eté*, *La Mer au plus près* (*The Sea close by*). Clamence is not, as he readily admits, capable of forgiving those who have offended him. He is so wrapped up in himself that he simply forgets what has happened. Occasionally, as he says, 'someone who thought I hated him could not recover from his surprise when I greeted him with a broad smile'. Camus, writing in his own name, describes in *La Mer au plus près* how 'Men praise me, I dream a little, they insult me and I am scarcely surprised. Then I forget, and I smile at someone who has insulted me, or greet someone I like with too much ceremony.' From a superficial point of view, this aspect of Clamence's behaviour is not unattractive. It is certainly likely to make other people less unhappy than the conduct of those whose religion, as Clamence observes, 'consists of forgiving those who have trespassed against them, and do in fact forgive. But who never forget.'[112] It is only when Clamence explains why he forgets so easily that you realise that his own offence, from a Christian point of view, is even worse than a refusal to forgive. His whole personality is eaten up with the sin of spiritual pride.

Camus's use of details about his own personality and career, like the more or less direct quotations from his published work, made *La Chute* seem a very public confession of his own shortcomings. The fact that it also seemed to be a confession couched in Christian terms added to its appeal. It gave an extra dimension to Camus's literary personality at the same time as it provided encouragement to those readers who were tempted to say of him, as Polyeucte says of Pauline in Corneille's *Polyeucte*, that she had too many virtues not to be a Christian.[113] But it was not only the references to Christianity which made *La Chute* fit in with the ongoing ideological debates of the French intellectual world. Like all Camus's novels, it was at one and the same time the expression of a particular stage in his intellectual autobiography and a work aimed very consciously at influencing the way he thought his contemporaries saw the world.

All Camus's major works, with the possible exception of *L'Etranger*, were indeed very much written with a contemporary French readership in mind. The thinkers criticised in *Le Mythe de Sisyphe* – Kierkegaard, Kafka, Jaspers, Husserl, Chestov – had recently become fashionable in French literary circles, and the essay on the absurd was an immediate contribution to an ongoing debate. Pascal, whose wager argument is an early version of the leap into faith argument, is mentioned only in passing, although Camus knew his work well.[114] The evocation in *La Peste* of the German occupation of France gave the book such an instant appeal to the readers of 1947 that some critics said that it would, to the readers of 2047, be as incomprehensible as the seventeenth-century pastoral novel *L'Astrée* is to readers today. *L'Homme révolté* argued that the respect for the individual which inspires all initial movements of revolt is lost as soon as revolutionaries seek total power, and illustrated this idea principally by the example of Marxism. This was, in the Paris of the early 1950s, a more widely accepted philosophy than it has since become, and Camus's attack on it seemed positively blasphemous to a large number of his readers. *L'Homme révolté* also included long essays on the then very fashionable figures in the French literary world of the Marquis de Sade and Antoine de Saint-Just. It dwelt in some detail on the writers of the essentially Paris-based surrealist movement as well as dealing with the very popular French poets Rimbaud and Lautréamont. Indeed, it is often so very French a book in some of its preoccupations and references as to be quite difficult to understand when removed from the intellectual climate against which it was directed.

There is also a sense in which Camus can be seen, throughout his career, as trying to compensate by discussing the most up-to-date Parisian writers for the fact that he came from the remotest and least intellectual part of France. This is certainly a possible explanation for his choice to discuss certain authors rather than others in *Le Mythe de Sisyphe* and *L'Homme révolté*, and the fact that not everyone then accepted him as the man who had come to put them providentially right could also have been a factor in the disillusionment which comes through both in *La Chute* and in the remarks he made in his own name in the 1950s. His impatience with the intellectual climate of mid-twentieth-century France certainly becomes very noticeable during the period leading up to the publication of *La Chute*, and sometimes recalls the attitude of two earlier writers from the provinces. Jean-Jacques Rousseau was not entirely happy in eighteenth-century Paris, and D. H. Lawrence had some strong reservations about the Bloomsbury set. While *La Chute* makes the same kind of assumption as *Le Mythe de Sisyphe* or *L'Homme révolté* about the knowledge which Camus's readers will have of the issues involved, it is also shot through with a disillusionment about his inability to change the intellectual climate of his day which strikes a new note in Camus's work. The Christian echoes which it contains are closely linked to the gloomier, Jansenistic version of the faith which has always made a particular appeal to the French.

Clamence explains that he had, in the days when he was a well-known *avocat* in Paris, a particular speciality: noble causes. He was the perpetual defender of the widow and the orphan, the man who could always be relied upon to sign a manifesto on behalf of the oppressed, the tireless verbal scourge of acts of injustice wherever they were committed. Even more than the reference to his capacity to combine dancing well in nightclubs with writing impressively intellectual books, it was this feature of Clamence's past career which enabled the critics and readers of 1956 immediately to see him as far more of a portrait of Camus himself than Meursault had ever been. The habit of siding with the oppressed, of coming out in favour of the more obvious values of justice and humanity, had always been Camus's own speciality. He had defended Michel Hodent, written eloquently and at length about the fate of the Arabs in Algeria, taken part in the resistance movement, denounced the dropping of the atom bomb on Hiroshima, castigated the ferocity with which the French government had put down the revolt in Madagascar in 1947, appealed for clemency on behalf of the Greek Communists sentenced to death in 1949, given some publicity to his resignation from UNESCO in 1952 to protest against the admission of Franco's Spain, made a public speech in June 1953 to condemn the shooting down in East Berlin of the workers demonstrating against the Communist régime, and pleaded with both sides in the Algerian war to respect the civilian population.

It is true, and this was the burden of Sartre's criticism of him when the two men quarrelled publicly in the columns of *Les Temps Modernes* in August 1952, that none of these denunciations was particularly difficult to make. They did not involve a decision as to which might be the lesser of two evils. The need to make such a choice had been in everyone's mind from November 1954 onwards. For the outbreak of the Algerian war had confronted everyone in France who took politics at all seriously with a very clear set of alternatives. They could support independence for Algeria and thus require the European settlers to leave their homes; or they could maintain the right of these Europeans to live where they wanted, and thus perpetuate the system whereby the Algerian Arabs were exploited and humiliated in their own country. It was a choice which Camus himself had deliberately refused to make, with the result that the rather ostentatiously moral stance which he had taken on earlier issues had been somewhat devalued. The protests against injustice which had been his speciality now seemed to his critics, as Clamence put it when speaking of the respects we pay to the dead, 'easy to fit in between a cocktail party and an attractive mistress'. In the article which he wrote after Camus's death, Sartre said that 'this Cartesian of the absurd refused to leave the certain terrain of morality and embark upon the uncertain paths of political action'.[115] The implied criticism of himself which he put into Clamence's monologue shows that Camus was not unaware of how vulnerable his failure to take sides on really contentious issues had now rendered him.

La Chute is also, of course, a work of fiction. Not everything in it has its origins in Camus's personal experience, even though Adèle King discovered that there actually is a Mexico City bar in Amsterdam; that it was managed, in the 1950s, by a muscular ex-sailor who spoke only Dutch; and that Camus so appreciated the opportunity of writing *La Chute* in the atmosphere it provided that he sent the management a copy.[116] But in spite of the reference in *Le Mythe de Sisyphe* to the idea that we might, quite by accident, be responsible for causing somebody to commit suicide by talking to them in an indifferent tone of voice, there is absolutely no evidence that Camus himself was ever involved in anything like the incident which makes Clamence realise how much of a whited sepulchre he is. In *Le Mythe de Sisyphe*, Camus's aim is to make a philosophical point about the knife edge we live on, in an absurd world between exaltation and despair. It also reflects the obsession with suicide that pursued Camus throughout his life. The illustrative anecdote which provides the narrative centre of *La Chute* makes a more moral point about the nature of moral responsibility.

One evening, as he is crossing the Seine by the Pont des Arts, feeling particularly pleased with himself, Clamence notices a young woman standing on the bridge looking into the river. A few moments later, he hears a splash, but does not behave as his ideal self-image might be expected to lead him to act. He does not dash back to the spot where he had last seen the girl, tear off his coat, dive into the water, and bring her young body triumphantly to safety. He does not, in other words, put on the show of virtue which normally leads him to offer help to motorists in distress, guide blind people across the road, or stand up to offer his seat to his fellow passengers in the bus or métro. There is nobody watching. The water is cold. Diving into the Seine late at night is not devoid of risks. Having crossed the river, he passes by on the other side.

Clamence tries to forget what has happened and makes a point, during the next few days, of not reading the newspapers. But the incident preys on his mind, and he begins to have the uncomfortable experience of hearing somebody laughing at him behind his back. He has in fact, according to French law, committed a crime: that of 'non-assistance à personne en danger', failing to go to the help of someone in danger. The memory of his failure lingers with him, and he becomes increasingly aware of other occasions in his past in which he has failed to live up to his own ideal self-image. One of these events in particular, a minor incident at a set of traffic lights, in which he is physically humiliated in public but lacks the courage to do anything about it, not only makes him realise that he is a coward; it also makes him aware, as he himself puts it, 'that every intelligent man dreams of being a gangster and of reigning over society by violence alone'. He becomes more and more conscious of how self-centred his earlier exercise of virtue had been, and expresses his discovery in an epigram which, for the French reader, has the ring of one of the more pessimistic maxims of La Rochefoucauld: 'Man is made like this, two-faced: he cannot love without loving himself.'[117]

In Genesis 3:7–8, Adam and Eve hide from God because they know that they are naked. They have yielded to temptation and eaten the fruit of the forbidden tree. Their reward has been the awareness that they have done wrong. This, in Christian theology, is what the Fall means. It is the act whereby man disobeys God, and thus becomes an essentially sinful being. It is, at one and the same time, the act of sin and our coming to awareness of it. This is why Camus, knowing that his readership, even in a country which had been a secular republic since 1905, still knew the basic doctrines of Christianity, gave his second *récit* the title of *La Chute*. In it, a man who is surprisingly and publicly very like himself, acknowledges that all his most apparently virtuous acts have been inspired by the sin of spiritual pride.

To anyone who has read *Noces*, *L'Etranger*, *Le Mythe de Sisyphe*, *La Peste* and *L'Homme révolté*, a confession couched in such ostentatiously Christian terms comes as something of a surprise. The notion of sin, in the pagan world of the first cycle of Camus's work, is totally meaningless. Meursault is prepared to admit that he has done wrong. He refuses to accept that he is a sinner. Such a confession is meaningful only within a world governed by a Christian God and redeemed by Christ. Meursault does not believe in God, and the face he can see in his prison walls, as he tells the chaplain, is not that of the suffering Christ but of Marie, and it has 'the colour of the sun and the flame of desire'.[118] In *La Peste*, human beings do harm to one another because they are misled by false ideas, not because they are sinful. The whole argument of *L'Homme révolté*, the central philosophical work of the second cycle, is that God is either non-existent, evil or incomprehensible, and that the only possible source of goodness in the universe is man himself.

La Chute consequently seems an ideological U-turn in Camus's career, especially since so many of its other references are to a specifically Christian way of thinking and feeling and even to an exclusively Christian vision of the natural and supernatural world. The canals in Amsterdam are compared to the concentric circles of Dante's hell, where both Clamence and his listener are in the second circle, that of the traitors. There is considerable nostalgia for Christ, and a reference to the limbo into which Dante admits the angels who were neutral in the war between God and Satan. This recalls T. S. Eliot's use of a comparable passage from *The Inferno* in *The Waste Land*. The crowd which flows over London Bridge is made up of those who have lived without praise or blame, and who are excluded from the possibility of salvation because they have no concept either of good or of evil. The same theme runs through the work of such specifically Roman Catholic novelists as François Mauriac, Graham Greene and Evelyn Waugh, and Clamence's confession seems deliberately aimed at characters such as Mauriac's Bernard Desqueyroux, the barmaid Ida in *Brighton Rock* or Rex Mottram in *Brideshead Revisited*. All three of them, albeit in their different ways, have the same absence of a sense of sin which enabled Clamence to feel so virtuous in the early part of his career, before the Fall. They would all, within a

Christian framework, benefit from listening to Clamence's confession, since it would reveal to each one of them how suspect their confidence in their own virtue really is. In writing a novel in which, as in *La Chute*, the central character discovers the reality of his own and of other people's sin, Camus could even be seen as joining the ranks of the twentieth-century Catholic novelists who have so effectively disproved George Orwell's assertion that since the novel as we know it is 'the product of rationalism, of the Protestant centuries, of the autonomous individual', Catholics on the whole 'have not excelled' at prose fiction.[119] Like Greene, Mauriac and Waugh, the Camus of 1956 seemed on the point of becoming a novelist whose principal aim was to show his readers that they had left undone the things they ought to have done, done the things that they ought not to have done, and that there was no health in them.

The temptation to interpret *La Chute* in Christian terms is indeed a strong one. Conor Cruise O'Brien stated in 1970 that '*La Chute* is profoundly Christian in its confessional form, in its imagery and above all in its pervasive message that it is only through the full recognition of our sinful nature that we can hope for grace', and added an interesting piece of information in a footnote. When, in 1957, he reviewed *The Fall* in its English translation, Camus 'wrote to his English publishers, Hamish Hamilton, confirming that this approach was sound'.[120]

There is no reason to doubt this. Camus's extremely pleasant nature led him to agree with most interpretations of his work which were based upon a conscientious reading. Some of his more public statements, however, suggest that he did not intend *La Chute* to be read as a Christian novel, and give force to the otherwise rather baffling entry in his *Carnets* for 1949: 'Toute mon œuvre est ironique' (the whole of my work is ironic).[121] In an interview in *Le Monde* on 31 August 1956, he pointed out that Clamence describes himself as being 'Sicilian and Javanese', and not Christian at all. Speaking in his own name, Camus said that he shared Clamence's friendship for 'the first of the Christians', and admired the fashion in which Christ both lived and died. His lack of imagination, he added, prevented him from going any further. An alternative title to *La Chute*, he said, had been 'A hero of our time', and Camus made it clear what he meant by the 'Prière d'insérer' (Note for critics) which accompanied the book. Clamence, he said, 'has a modern heart, that is to say that he cannot bear to be judged. He therefore hastens to make out a case against himself, but this is in order better to judge other people.'[122]

Unlike some of Camus's comments on *L'Etranger*, this way of looking at *La Chute* fits everything in the text. Clamence does indeed confess his sins, but not to obtain absolution. He is totally different from the Catholic priest who, on giving absolution, is required to say 'Forgive me, for I too have sinned.' Clamence's sole aim in describing his own imperfection is to compel his listener to recognise that he too is guilty of the same sins. Clamence tries to do this because, as he recognises, he has always hated being judged and always wanted to look down on other people. The only way to retain this superiority is for him to be the first to realise what the true situation is. By starting off with a revelation of his own sins, he gives himself the advantage of being first in the field. He can thus doubly despise those who have listened to him and been infected by his eloquence: he can look down on them because they are sinners; he can patronise them because, without his help, they would have never discovered the truth about themselves.

Not even Camus's most hostile critics have cast doubt upon the qualities of style and composition either of *L'Etranger* or of *La Peste*. *La Chute* offers a comparable perfection of form as well as an equal mastery of the spirit of place. Instead of the dazzling sun, bright colours and clear light of Algeria, *La Chute* offers the mist, fogs and rain of Amsterdam, with its sea 'steaming like a laundry', and its only light the warm but artificial glow of the alcohol consumed in its murky bars. The short, precise sentences in which Meursault noted down the exact detail of his physical sensations have given way to the complex verbal structures in which Clamence, sitting there like a spider spinning its web, endeavours to ensnare his victim. The slightly detached tone in which Meursault recorded the oddities of his own and other people's behaviour has disappeared. Instead, we have humour of a more sardonic nature as Clamence observes how some of his clients had committed crimes solely in order to see their name in the papers. 'To become known,' he comments, 'all you need to do is kill your concierge. Unfortunately, this is an ephemeral reputation, since there are so many concierges who deserve to have their throat cut and to whom this happens.'[123] Camus once said that the quality which critics had most neglected in his work was its humour.[124] *La Chute* is one of the best texts to study from this point of view, especially when Clamence, intending to play down a charitable action he has performed, is led by a slip of the tongue to say that nobody would have done the same thing when he intended to say anybody. Camus also said that if he had not been a writer, he would have liked to be a sculptor. Like *L'Etranger*, *La Chute* shows him modelling a person and a place until they are in complete harmony with each other. You cannot imagine Meursault elsewhere than in a Mediterranean seaport, and more particularly Algiers. Take Clamence away from Camus's Amsterdam, and you take away half his life. Unless, of course, you put him back in Paris.

La Chute is the only one of Camus's major works to be set even partially in metropolitan France. Of the six short stories in *L'Exil et le royaume*, only 'Jonas ou l'artiste au travail' (The artist at work) takes place in Paris, and its autobiographical features offer an interesting contrast to *La Chute* in the alternative version which they provide of how Camus saw himself in his later years. *La Chute* is, however, a Parisian novel in the principal target for its satire. Like Camus's other novels, it has an appeal which stretches beyond the narrow streets of St Germain-des-Prés. By raising the general problem of whether or not all virtuous actions are somehow rendered valueless by the satisfaction given to us by the knowledge that we are doing good, it again shows what a very good writer for sixth forms Camus never ceased to be. However difficult they may find *La Chute* on first reading, it is a good thing for adolescents to discuss questions of this kind before settling down to the serious business either of violent revolution or of chartered accountancy. There must surely have been one or two widows and orphans whose lot was slightly eased by the interest Clamence took in their affairs, and it would be very odd to argue that we should not stop to help somebody whose car has broken down simply because the satisfaction we feel in helping him to get it going again might make us feel rather too pleased with ourselves. In English-speaking countries, much of Camus's appeal as a moralist has stemmed from the way the cult of effort in *Le Mythe de Sisyphe*, like the insistence upon personal responsibility in *La Peste* and *L'Homme révolté*, echoes certain aspects of the Protestant tradition. *La Chute* invites us to think more critically about the equally Protestant notion that acts can be virtuous only if they cost us pain to perform.

It is not only for Christians that *La Chute* raises the question of how we should react to the discovery, which does not always come as quite so much of a surprise to everybody else as it seems to have done to Clamence, that we are not so good as we thought we were. In his reluctance to be judged, Clamence is a pathological case. But Camus may have been drawing on what he himself had felt during the polemics which followed the publication of *L'Homme révolté*, and Clamence's reaction is only a more extreme version of what we all feel when we are criticised. Just as *La Peste* and *L'Homme révolté* urge the virtues of moderation and scepticism in political matters, so *La Chute* can be read as a book which makes us think critically about the extremes both of genuine guilt and of attempted innocence. I first heard the name of Camus in the chapel of King's College London, in 1949, only a year after the translation of *La Peste* had appeared in English. There would always, Canon Eric Abbott told us, be rats coming out to die on the pavements of happy cities. Human sinfulness was a permanent condition and consequently a permanent threat. It was not a bad idea for undergraduates to contemplate, however irresistible their subsequent agnosticism may have proved to be. The problem of whether or not we are all miserable sinners, and what we ought to do about it if we are, is not without interest even nowadays.

One of the most intriguing aspects of Camus's whole work is how frequently he wrote about problems within a Christian framework. Critics eager to annex even the most determined agnostic to their own particular version of Christianity, find this easy to explain. It is a sign that Camus never ceased to feel guilty, consciously or unconsciously, at having abandoned the faith in which he had been brought up and which he had chosen to study in some detail as a young man. Like St Augustine, such critics argue, he had a naturally Christian soul (*anima naturaliter Christiana*) and could not therefore cast off all nostalgia for the true faith. Had his life not been cut so tragically short, they suggest, he would certainly have ended up in the Church.

It is nevertheless possible to see the recurrence of Christian themes in Camus's work in a more historical and less personal context. He observed in *L'Homme révolté* that Nietzsche's famous remark that 'God is dead' should not be seen as referring to something which had happened outside space and time. It was, he argued, a recognition that religious faith was dead in the here and now, an acknowledgement that fewer and fewer people believed in God in any real sense.[125] When you look at Camus's fiction from this point of view, it certainly bears out the general validity of this interpretation. At the same time, however, it reminds us very forcibly of how long a phenomenon such as Christianity takes to disappear. The values by which Meursault lives and dies have to be expressed as a conscious defiance of Christian ideology because there is no other contrast by which they can be made clear. It is only because Camus's readers are aware of Christianity as a religion which preaches the sinfulness of man, his redemption by Christ, and his consequent immortality that Meursault's refusal to see himself as a sinner, his disbelief in Christ and his lack of interest in immortality mark him out as a particular kind of outsider. If Christianity had never preached the doctrines of the fatherhood of God and of divine intervention in human history, both Paneloux's sermons would be totally meaningless. The idea that the world has no transcendent purpose has to be couched in Christian terms because only the Christians say it has such a purpose. If Clamence's name were not an ironic echo of John 1:23 – the voice of one crying in the wilderness; cf. Isaiah 40:3 – *La Chute* would be fairly meaningless; and to readers unacquainted with the Christian doctrine of man's sinfulness, the aim of Clamence's confession would be incomprehensible. Camus had to present his ideas in Christian terms because there is still, in the late twentieth century, no equally accessible world view available. It does not mean he believed in them, any more than the tools which Robinson Crusoe found in the wreck of the boat were the ones he would personally have chosen. God may be dead, in several senses of the word. But His ghost is taking a long time to disappear.

At first sight, it might seem to limit the appeal and interest of *La Chute* to stop seeing it in these broad historical terms and replace it in the immediate context of the intellectual atmosphere of Paris in 1956. Camus's original intention, as he explained in *Le Monde* on 31 August 1956, was to 'draw a portrait, that of a minor prophet of the kind that are so frequent nowadays. They announce nothing at all and find nothing better to do than to accuse others while accusing themselves.'[126] If, as has been suggested, one of the prophets that Camus had in mind was Jean-Paul Sartre, there is some evidence in Sartre's own work for the accuracy of Camus's diagnosis. In 1952, the same year as the quarrel about *L'Homme révolté*, Sartre published a long book called *Saint Genet, comédien et martyr*. It was a study of the novels of Jean Genet, a French writer who had spent his life in and out of jail, who made no secret of the fact that he had been put into prison for theft and drug smuggling, who appeared to glory in having betrayed his accomplices to the police, and who presented himself as an active and enthusiastic homosexual. Sartre's conclusion, at the end of some five hundred closely written pages, was that the 'honest citizen' who picked up one of Genet's novels to 'see what it's all about' would rapidly become trapped into feeling the emotions that Genet described.[127] Like the listener who happened to bump into Clamence in the Mexico City bar, this reader would then fairly rapidly be brought to the point where he recognised that the reason why he responded so sympathetically to Genet's account of the delights of homosexuality and theft was that this account had awoken aspects of his personality whose existence he had not earlier suspected. 'For the Colonel's Lady an' Judy O'Grady', as Kipling remarked in *The Ladies*, 'Are sisters under their skins!' The effect of reading Genet, or of listening to Clamence, is to make the colonel appreciate how much he has in common with the gentleman ranker – or even the private soldier – whom he might earlier have despised.

There is no evidence that Camus ever read *Saint Genet, comédien et martyr*. One of the charges which Sartre made against him in 1952 was that he had no first-hand knowledge of any of the authors discussed in *L'Homme révolté*, and he added: 'I shall at least have this in common with Hegel, that you have read neither of us.'[128] In 1952, Camus also wrote a long letter to a critic with the initials P. B. explaining how very difficult he found it to read all the books he wanted to and see all the friends he liked, and there is an echo of these feelings of dissatisfaction with himself in the way he makes Clamence describe his life as 'filled with half read books and with half seen friends'.[129] But he would have been familiar with the basic assumption about bourgeois guilt lying behind Sartre's 'Prière pour le bon usage de Genet' (Please Use Genet Properly), and it is not uncommon to find aspects of Sartre's argument in left-wing circles even today. For if, in England, you read the *Guardian* – *né* 'The Manchester Guardian' – the *New Statesman* or *New Society*, you will find that the overall effect of the articles and news items they contain is to make you feel guilty. Everybody is unhappy and it is all your fault. Sometimes, when the author of the article adds that it is her or his fault as well, you almost hear Clamence talking.

You can find a similar obsession with guilt running through a French left-wing journal such as *Le Nouvel Observateur*, and the attitude was even more marked in the 1950s. Things were going badly in France, with the Algerian war breaking out within three months of the end of the eight-year war by which the French had rather spectacularly failed to hang on to their colonial empire in Indochina. Governments were unstable and uncertain, the economy was in poor shape, and France itself generally regarded in the foreign press as the sick man of Europe. If, however, you were politically on the left, and more particularly if you were sympathetic to the Communist Party, you could see this gloom and doom as merely signs of the darkest hour before the dawn. You could recognise that it was all the fault of the middle class. This class had strangled the resistance movement before it had had time to put its social programme into effect, and was now pursuing a colonialist war in Algeria which showed exactly how right Lenin had been to describe imperialism as capitalism in its final phase. But – and here lay your chance of social as well as personal salvation – you could see that even the middle class could contribute to the end of all this misery. All that its members had to do was admit that it was their fault. They would then be quite happy to accept, as a salutary and well-deserved punishment for their misdeeds, the austere discipline and temporary reduction in personal freedom which the Party would find it necessary to introduce as a brief prelude to the singing tomorrows.

When Camus makes Clamence say 'You see in me, *très cher*, an enlightened prophet of slavery', he is addressing a fairly broad wink at any reader who shares his own view of the left as a movement whose members are inspired largely by the desire to boss other people about. In 1958, he published under the title of *Actuelles III* a collection of the articles he had written on Algeria, from 1939 to 1956. He presented it as his final attempt to bring about a solution to the Algerian problem, and may well have been disappointed at what looks curiously like the conspiracy of silence which greeted it in the French press. In his *Avant-Propos*, however, he made a very Clamence-like remark about people who 'went with no transition at all from speeches about honour and brotherhood to the worship of the *fait accompli* and of the cruellest party'.[130] Clamence, too, spoke about the people who 'go in for politics and run directly to the cruellest party', and it is quite instructive to go through the essays and articles which Camus wrote in the 1950s, as well as through his *Carnets* for the same period, and see how often he makes Clamence-type remarks in his own name. It reminds you that *La Chute*, again like *L'Etranger*, does not have to be read only by one code. It was originally intended to be one of the short stories in *L'Exil et le royaume*. Then, as Camus worked on it, he became increasingly absorbed in its atmosphere and themes, to the point where it is only twelve pages shorter than *L'Etranger*. This may well be because he was genuinely haunted by an awareness of his own inadequacies, and wished to exorcise his feelings of guilt by casting them into a work of art. You can therefore see it as a confession, albeit of a subtler and more interesting kind than the autobiographical works of Alfred de Musset.

It is equally possible to see its length as a reflection of Camus's awareness, as an artist, that he was on to a very good thing. No writer, especially one as haunted as Camus was in the last years of his life by the danger of artistic sterility, could turn his nose up at the excellent copy which Clamence provided, whether this originated in his own personality or in the society around him. Like Meursault, Clamence is one of the best-known and most intriguing characters in twentieth-century French literature. Like the hero of *L'Etranger*, and like Rieux, Grand and Tarrou in *La Peste*, he draws his fascination to a considerable extent from the expression which he provides for Camus's own dilemmas and from Camus's debate with himself. When *La Chute* was published, readers went to it first and foremost in order to see what Camus thought about things now. The answer, although ambiguous, was not disappointing.

Like *L'Etranger*, *La Chute* also contains some intriguing problems for which, by the very nature of literature, there can be no certain solution. Just as we cannot know exactly why Meursault fires four additional shots into the Arab's body, or when he writes down the first-person narrative which seems to end with his death, so there are areas of Clamence's story which are primarily invitations to the reader to use his own imagination. His full name, Jean-Baptiste Clamence, is clearly intended to evoke John the Baptist. He makes the point himself, adding that he has no intention, unlike the prophet sent to bear witness of that Light (John 1:8), of ever leaving the wilderness. But Clamence also evokes 'clémence', mercy, the quality in which he is so conspicuously lacking. In any case, he adds, it is not his real name, so you could think of him in quite different terms. There is some complicated symbolism in his constant reference to the picture *Les Juges intègres* (*The Upright Judges*) which he keeps in his room, and which links up with the leitmotiv of the law and of lawyers which provides one of the central strands of the book. Since Clamence is the only person to know that the genuine original of this picture is the one in this room, he can rejoice in the fact that false judges are being held up for people's admiration while he alone knows the truth. His story of how he was elected Pope in a displaced persons' camp may be pure invention. As he suggests on a number of occasions, everything he says may be a tissue of lies, and Camus may, as Roger Quilliot suggests, be exploring Cocteau's paradox of the imaginative writer who tells lies in order better to bring out the truth. One of the defining characteristics of great works of art is that no set of interpretations can ever exhaust their wealth. This is even the case for a book which, like *La Chute*, can also be read as a very straightforward moral fable about the dangers of excess, of what the Camus of *L'Homme révolté* called 'la démesure'. Had Clamence been less extreme in his self-satisfaction before his fall, his reaction to it would not have taken the violent form which it did. Fundamental to Camus's analysis in *L'Homme révolté* of the transformation of revolt into tyranny is the idea that this transformation might be avoided by the exercise of moderation. This, too, if one links *La Chute* to Camus's other works, is true of Clamence's attitude to guilt. A more positive reading of *La Chute* is as a novel which suggests how we might become adults in an attitude to other people's guilt as well as to our own. All we need to do – it is easier in theory than in practice – is learn to look at our virtues and vices with the same ironic detachment.

5

Exile, Humanism and a Conclusion

All the characters in the six short stories which make up the last book of fiction which Camus published, *L'Exil et le royaume*, suffer from geographical or spiritual exile, and sometimes from both. In the first, *La Femme adultère* (*The Adulterous Woman*), Janine and her husband Marcel are Europeans travelling in the southern regions of Algeria. They may not, in Camus's view, have been in a country which was not legally or politically their own. They are shopkeepers in one of the Algerian coastal towns, members of the community whose interests Camus was concerned to protect. But the story insists on how out of place they look and feel in what one is tempted to call the real Algeria of the high plateaux, and Marcel's attitude towards the Arabs they meet is one of typically colonialist superiority and suspicion. But Janine, the only woman to occupy a central position in Camus's fiction, also suffers from a deeper and more serious sense of exile. She feels that her body has become heavy and clumsy with age, and looks back nostalgically at the lithe and athletic girl she was in her youth.

The action of the second story, *Le Renégat et l'esprit confus* (*The Renegade*) also takes place in Africa. It too has a European as its main character, an unusual missionary whose tragic misadventures are told in Camus's one attempt at an experimental technique of narration. An excited interior monologue, made more confused because the missionary's tongue has been cut out and there is 'une bouillie' (a jumble of words) in his head, tells of his initial conversion from Protestantism to Roman Catholicism, of his subsequent desire to convert the heathen, of his failure to do so and consequent espousal of their own cruel gods. As a native of the Massif Central, the mountainous, wooded region into which Camus was sent to recover from a recurrence of his tuberculosis in 1943, he is totally in exile in the burning sands of the southern Sahara. He is also, perhaps more importantly, in total exile from the spirit of tolerance which it has become customary in the late twentieth century to see as one of the major virtues of Christianity.

The third story, *Les Muets* (*The Silent Men*) resembles the first in depicting the Europeans of French Algeria at work. In 1954, the publication in the volume entitled *L'Eté* of a number of essays written between 1939 and 1953 had given the impression that Camus's vision of the French Algerians had changed little since the days of *Noces*. They were still the easy-going, uncomplicated pagans whose warmth and friendliness contrasted so favourably with the coldness of the Northern Europeans. They also seemed untroubled either by the presence of nine million Arabs in what they saw as their country or by any class conflicts among themselves. *La Femme adultère* and *Les Muets* change at least one aspect of this idyllic picture, if not perhaps the most important one. Marcel is having difficulty with his business, and has come to the South in order to make what he hopes will be a quick profit by selling cloth to the natives. Since the attention in the story moves much more towards his wife, we do not find out whether he is successful in this or not. Yvars, the central character in *Les Muets*, has just taken part in an unsuccessful strike. Because the wooden wine casks they make cannot compete with new forms of bulk transport, he and his fellow workmen have had to accept the low wages offered by a declining industry. Their defeat has made them sullen, and they refuse to speak to their employer. When this employer's child falls ill, they realise how exiled they have become from the comradeship which is one of the most important rewards that work can offer.

Like Janine, Yvars is also very aware that he is growing old. The pleasures of youth, which are very much those celebrated in *Noces*, are becoming increasingly closed to him. He can no longer swim and cycle as he did when he was young, and he is experiencing what Camus also described in *Noces* as the inevitable counterpart of a life wholly dominated by the senses. 'A workman of thirty', he wrote in 'Summer in Algiers' in 1938, 'has already played all his cards. He waits for the end with his wife and children around him.'[131] By showing this happening to Yvars, and by describing a comparable change in Janine, Camus is exploring the darker side of the coin whose more shining face had

given Meursault the 'poorest but most certain' of his joys. At the
same time, he is also telling his readers in metropolitan France
that not all the European Algerians are fascist beasts or colonialist
profiteers. They are exactly like people anywhere else, and *L'Exil
et le royaume* marked a new departure in Camus's work by
describing characters who are rather more run of the mill than
Meursault, Tarrou or Clamence. In his first two cycles, as he
observed in his *Carnets* for 1950, Camus realised that he had not
been a novelist in the usual meaning of the word but rather 'an
artist who creates myths on the scale of his passion and
anguish'.[132] Although *La Chute* might be seen as representing the
third cycle, that of a creative revival in which he chose his subjects
for their aesthetic potentialities, Clamence is still somewhat larger
than life. It is not given to everyone to be exiled from innocence in
quite such a dramatic way. In all but one of the stories in *L'Exil et
le royaume*, on the other hand, the characters react in a way which
might well be our own to their separation from the country in
which they would like to live. Only in *L'Esprit confus* do we feel the
presence of an unusual, quasi-mythical figure. Exile, the first of
the two themes of the title and illustrated with almost pedagogical
thoroughness by each of the stories, is not a metaphysical
experience. Unlike *Le Mythe de Sisyphe* or *L'Homme révolté*, which
have struck some English readers as too abstract to have much
immediate relevance to their own problems, the stories in *L'Exil et
le royaume* illustrate some of Camus's own major preoccupations by
exploring situations which are realistic in a fairly conventional
sense.

The title of the fourth story, *L'Hôte*, is a pun. Since, in French,
the word can mean either host or guest, the theme of exile differs
according to the interpretation chosen. If you take it to mean host,
the emphasis is on the European, the schoolteacher Daru. He is
given the task of looking after an Arab who has been arrested for
killing one of his relatives in a blood feud and who has to be
escorted to the prison in the nearest town. Daru is a schoolteacher
in a remote, mountainous area of Algeria, and again one of the
European Algerians whom Camus is presenting to his
countrymen in France as very much like themselves. He has been
born and brought up in Algeria, and 'felt in exile anywhere else'.
Like the other characters in Camus's fictional world, he doesn't
care for the police, and tells the gendarme, Balducci, that he won't
hand the Arab over to the authorities. Although he still has to

accept custody of him, he eats with him, takes no precautions against being attacked, and would probably be quite happy if the Arab escaped during the night.

The following morning, he takes him to a point where the Arab can choose. Either he can go to the town where the authorities are waiting for him, or he can take the day's walk which will bring him to the high plateau where the nomadic tribes will accept and shelter him. As Daru looks back, he sees the Arab walking steadily in the direction of the town. When he arrives back at the school, he sees written on the blackboard the words: 'You have handed over our brother. You will pay.' Daru looks at the sky, and towards the sea that lies beyond. 'In this vast country which he had loved so much, he was alone.'

If – like Justin O'Brien, who translated *L'Exil et le royaume* into English – you give the story the title of *The Guest*, the concept of exile is more disconcerting, especially to readers tempted to feel sympathy for Camus's attitude towards the Algerian war. Daru is presented as a very sympathetic character. The map he has drawn on the blackboard, with the four rivers of France flowing towards their estuaries, may illustrate the French-centred kind of education offered to the Arabs in Algeria. But Daru speaks Arabic to his prisoner, and would like to see him escape. The most you can say against him is that he is what the Tunisian writer Alfred Memmi accused Camus of being, 'le colonisateur de bonne volonté', the well-intentioned coloniser.[133] The best of us, with his situation and background, would not do any better. The Arab, in contrast, is rather stupid, and even slightly bestial. He has thick lips, and clearly does not understand the question when Daru asks him if he regrets having slit his cousin's throat with a billhook. His refusal to escape to the nomadic tribes and decision to go instead to the town where he knows that he will be put in prison and probably executed suggests that he is in no way ready for the freedom which his fellow countrymen are preparing to obtain by violence. Balducci talks about an imminent uprising, Daru is prepared to fight if it takes place, and the writing that suddenly appears on the blackboard suggests a situation where the Europeans are under constant watch from an enemy they can't see. But the man whom the Arab revolutionaries are clearly preparing to present as a martyr to the revolution – 'Tu as trahi notre frère' – is depicted as being in deeper intellectual and moral exile than anyone else in Camus's work. His notions of right and wrong make Meursault seem a positive paragon of moral sensitivity. His sense of where his true interests might lie is totally non-existent.

As though in deliberate contrast to this highly pessimistic account of personal and political relationships in French Algeria, the next story in *L'Exil et le royaume* is written with a lightness of touch which justifies Camus's complaint that critics of his work always neglected its humorous side. 'Jonas ou l'artiste au travail' is about a painter whose success as an artist places him in the paradoxical position where he is increasingly unable to practise his art. This particular form of exile is caused partly by the fact that he doesn't do quite well enough to be able to rent a studio. He therefore has to work at home, where his wife and children also have to live their lives. But his exile is also brought about by the presence of the innumerable hangers-on whom his generous nature prevents him from telling to get lost, and by that of the disciples who – like the innumerable critics writing about Camus – 'explained to him at length what he had painted and why'. This enables Jonas – like Camus himself, no doubt, when reading the studies of his books – to discover in his paintings 'a host of intentions that rather surprised him, and a host of things he had not put there',[134] but it does not help him to paint any pictures. Eventually, in order to escape from everyone, he builds a little eyrie for himself way up in the high rooms of his apartment, whose proportions are remarkably similar to those which Camus once lived in with his wife and two children. Jonas disappears into this hideaway and devotes himself to painting a picture which consists of one, slightly curious word. You cannot tell whether it is 'solitaire' (alone) or 'solidaire' (at one with other people).

The message of *Jonas ou l'artiste au travail* is thus a very clear one: the artist will best show his solidarity with the rest of humanity by devoting himself in solitude to his calling as an artist. This is an unexceptionable idea, and the fact that Camus had to state it at all is more informative about the poisons and delights of French intellectual life in the 1950s than it is about art itself. Everyone agrees that this is an activity which needs a great deal of peace and quiet. From 1943, Camus became a reader at the publishing house of Gallimard, and was still employed there when he was killed. The regular salary which he received enabled him to avoid the danger of ever having to write and publish a book because he needed the money. Such an arrangement is common practice in the French literary world. It did nevertheless mean that he had to live in Paris, a city he seems to have disliked, and to keep abreast of everything which was happening on the literary front.

In the 1940s and 1950s, the reigning orthodoxy in literary Paris was what was known at the time as 'la littérature engagée', committed literature. The principal tenets of this concept of literature were set out by Jean-Paul Sartre in *Qu'est-ce que la littérature?* in 1947, and a number of aspects of Camus's own work do show him putting into practice the idea that the writer should take sides in contemporary political issues. But he didn't think much of it as a literary ideal, and felt increasingly that it led to a wrong order of priorities. 'In 1957', he declared in his Nobel Prize lecture, 'Racine would apologize for writing *Bérénice* instead of protesting against the revocation of the Edict of Nantes', and the Biblical quotation at the beginning of *Jonas ou l'artiste au travail* makes the slightly implausible suggestion that the modern world feels such a hostility towards the artist that it would like to get rid of him altogether.[135] For Jonah 1:12 reads 'And he said unto them, Take me up, and cast me forth into the sea, . . . for I know that for my sake this great tempest is upon you.'

The quotation also invites the reader to see the artist as forced into a kind of inner exile by the pressures which society exerts on him. It is a providential exile, for it also enables the artist to recover his kingdom: the world in which he is free to create. But for all the humour of its opening section, *Jonas ou l'artiste au travail* suffers from the disadvantage apparently inseparable from all discussions of the nature of art: the picture by which Jonas finds a solution to his problems does not tell us about anything but art itself. The disadvantage of looking at Camus primarily as an artist, an approach which he said was most appropriate to the driving force behind his work, was succinctly expressed by the philosopher Jacques Derrida. What, he asked, would literature be if it was only itself? ('Que serait la littérature si elle n'était qu'elle-même, littérature?')[136]

Gilbert Jonas is the only character in Camus's work who is a Frenchman living and working in France. Unlike the other characters in *L'Exil et le royaume*, he is not therefore in any way a geographical exile. But like Camus himself, he nevertheless feels an exile in the particular section of French society in which he lives, and his final decision to seek refuge solely in his art runs parallel to Camus's remark in his *Carnets* for 1950: 'Yes, I do have

a country. The French language.' He is also the only one to be
married and have children, and there occasionally seems
something rather odd in the way Camus never found this
particular relationship an interesting one to explore in his novels
and plays. The central character in the final story in *L'Exil et le
royaume, La Pierre qui pousse*, is also a Frenchman, but he is
unmarried and has decided not to live in France. It is, he says, a
country where those who are masters over the people are
policemen and merchants, and he does not disagree with the
remark then made by the person he is talking to. This is that
buying and selling are filth ('Quelle saleté') and that with the
police 'it is the dogs who are in charge' ('avec la police, les chiens
commandent'). Like a number of contemporary writers, Camus
did not admire the wealth-creating capacity of capitalist society.
The question of where the people who bought his books found the
money to do so does not seem to have interested him. Neither does
he seem to have wondered what a society would be like in which
there was no police force to guard its citizens while they slept.
There is a simple explanation for this: in mid-twentieth-century
France, as in Europe in general, the police were often required to
play a political role. Quite a lot of people therefore came to think
that this was all they did. Camus's life-long enthusiasm for
revolutionary syndicalism led him to be one of them.

It is thus by choice that d'Arrast, the main character in *La Pierre
qui pousse*, is in exile. The action takes place in Brazil, where
d'Arrast, a civil engineer employed by a French company, has
gone to organise the building of a dam in a very poor part of the
country. The central anecdote describes how a ship's cook has
made a vow, if he were saved from a shipwreck, to carry a
fifty-kilo stone to the shrine of the Virgin Mary. But he cannot
resist the temptation to dance at the *macumba* which precedes the
feast day, and collapses before he can fulfil his promise. D'Arrast,
not himself a believer, then picks up the stone, but walks past the
church in the direction of the cook's house. When he has deposited
the stone in the fire which is burning at the centre of the room, the
cook's brother tells him to sit down at the empty place as a
member of the family.

The image on which *L'Exil et le royaume* closes is consequently
one of harmony and acceptance. D'Arrast has found his kingdom,
and it is one whose nature had been foreshadowed as early as 1943
when Camus had written in *Le Mythe de Sisyphe* that the only real

luxury was that of human relationships. Camus had also spoken in *La Peste* of 'ceux qui se contentent de l'homme et de son terrible et pauvre amour' (those whose desires are limited to man and to his humble yet formidable love),[137] and the first of the several kingdoms evoked in these six short stories is that of the communion of men united in some cause. This is why Yvars, in *Les Muets*, suffers so much from his form of exile. His ideal, which reflects Camus's own, is that of a group of men exercising their individual skills in co-operation with one another. Camus began his Nobel Prize lecture with the statement that art, for him, was not a cause of solitary rejoicing, and one of the reasons why he was so happy in the theatre was that it involved working with other people towards a common goal. Just as Yvars enjoys the difficult task of joining together the different planks of wood to make a watertight barrel, so Camus enjoyed exercising the skill which he had acquired as a typesetter. He was quite good at this, and in 1962, a group of typographers produced a book, *A Albert Camus, ses amis de livre*, as a tribute to his memory. The kingdom for Jonas, in *L'Artiste au travail*, is to paint pictures. But as the word which makes up his final painting shows, the art which he produces in solitude is the only way in which he can show solidarity with other people.

Part of the kingdom suggested by the title of the last work of fiction that Camus published thus lies in the realisation of an essentially humanist ideal. The idea that one of the highest forms of happiness lies in working together shows that the human solidarity against misfortune which inspires Tarrou's 'épiques sanitaires' is not simply a defence mechanism. It can take a more active and optimistic form as well, and another profession which Camus would have liked to exercise if he had not been an artist and journalist was that of schoolteacher.[138] But just as there are different forms of exile, so there are different kingdoms. *Les Muets* is Camus's one exploration of the world of ordinary work, and a tribute to one of his uncles on his mother's side of the family, who was a cooper actually called Etienne Yvars. While in no way a political work like *La Peste* or *L'Homme révolté*, *Les Muets* also hints at yet another defect in Marxism. Even in a socialist society, there will be technological changes which render certain skills obsolete. Yvars's kingdom is under constant threat from the ability of modern mass-production methods to make goods quickly and cheaply. The only hope for its preservation lies in the innovation mentioned in *L'Homme révolté* whereby one machine becomes so efficient that it enables one man to produce a highly complex object by himself. But Yvars's exile is even more irredeemable on a personal than it is on a professional level. Like Janine, in *La Femme adultère*, he is getting old.

Old age is a theme which occurs frequently in Camus's work. it is the great threat to the happiness of the young barbarians of *Noces*, and the first of the essays in *L'Envers et l'endroit*, *L'Ironie* (Irony), describes old people with considerable sympathy. One of the more attractive characteristics of Meursault, in *L'Etranger*, is his readiness to listen to the old man Salamano and his tales about his equally ancient dog. In his account of his mother's funeral, Meursault dwells in some detail on the behaviour of an old man, Pérez, a fellow inmate of the home in which his mother has just died. Because, in the evening of their lives, Pérez and Madame Meursault had gone for walks together and behaved almost as though they were engaged, he is allowed to follow her coffin to the church and subsequently to the cemetery. But it is a very hot day and the hearse travels too fast for him to keep up with it without almost running. In the end he faints, collapsing at the graveside 'like a dislocated marionette'. The total indifference to his welfare shown by the Director of the Old People's Home, who is present throughout the proceedings and does nothing to slow things down, makes the whole ceremony seem mechanical and hypocritical. However insensitive Meursault may appear, at least he notices when other people are uncomfortable.

Old age is also an important theme in Camus's later work because it is the great obstacle to any realisation of what he sees as the most important kingdom: the one offered by the harmony between man and the natural world. In one of the most striking images in *Noces*, he writes:

> I must be naked and dive into the sea, scented with the perfumes of the earth, wash these off in the sea, and consummate on my flesh the embrace for which sun and sea, lips to lips, have so long been sighing.[139]

This, if he had been gifted with Camus's powers of expression, is how Yvars might have described the pleasure which it gave him, as a young man, to dive into the 'deep, clear water' of the bay. But old age has deprived him of this pleasure, and he no longer even looks at the Mediterranean as he cycles past it on his way to work.

Janine's kingdom, which she finds at the very end of the story, is also one of union with the natural world, coupled with an affinity for the solitude and dignity of the nomads whom she and her husband see on their visit to the Sahara and its high plateaux. Like most of the French Algerians who lived in the coastal towns, she has no knowledge of Arabic. Both Balducci and Daru, in *L'Hôte*, speak to the Arab prisoner in his own language, and they would clearly not have been able to do their job unless they could do this. But for the Europeans in the towns, such an ability was rare, and there may be a hint of self-criticism on Camus's part in this reference to 'this language which she had heard spoken all her life without ever understanding it'.[140] He knew only a few words of Arabic, and none of his articles discusses the question of whether Arabic should be recognised as an administrative language in Algeria, and whether it should be given equal status with French.

This inability to communicate with them does not prevent Janine from envying 'these poverty-stricken but free lords of a strange kingdom' ('seigneurs misérables et libres d'un étrange royaume'). Her longing reflects Camus's own fascination for a life stripped to its bare essentials, and his dislike of a materialistic society. The word 'seigneur' also finds an echo later in the volume in d'Arrast's reference to his aristocratic lineage. The extreme poverty of Camus's background encouraged him, perhaps rather paradoxically, to feel a certain nostalgia for traditional aristocratic values. He spoke of honour as the one luxury still available to the poor, and disliked a society in which prestige was based principally on wealth. It is in this context that the sympathy for Spain which he expressed throughout his work takes on a different and broader social meaning. For Camus, it was in Mediterranean rather than Anglo-Saxon countries that aristocratic values could profit from the fact of not necessarily being linked with wealth.

The kingdom which Janine discovers at the end of the story nevertheless does not have anything to do with forms of social organisation. It is much more closely linked to the theme of man's physical union with the world, which provides one of the many similarities between *Noces* and *L'Etranger*. After exhausting his anger in his outburst against the prison chaplain, Meursault allows 'the marvellous peace of this sleeping summer' to flow into him like a tide, opens himself for the first time to what he calls 'the tender indifference of the world'. Janine has a comparably pantheistic experience of the world as she steals from her husband's bed in the middle of the night and stands, her stomach against the parapet of the fort, looking at the night and its garlands of stars.

> Then, with unbearable gentleness, the water of night began to fill Janine, drowned the cold, rose gradually from the hidden core of her being and overflowed in wave after wave, rising up even to her mouth full of moans. The next moment, the whole sky stretched out over her, fallen on her back on the cold earth.[141]

Her kingdom is thus very much of this world. It is even, if you choose to read the passage that way, intensely sexual in nature. It recalls the statement in *Noces* that 'embracing a woman's body also means holding in your arms this strange joy which descends from sky to sea', as well as the night-time swim in which Rieux and Tarrou finally free themselves of the town and of the disease and seal their friendship in *La Peste*. The essential innocence of Janine's communion with nature also shows how easily a shorter version of *La Chute* would have fitted into the atmosphere of *L'Exil et le royaume*. The guilt-ridden Clamence is inhabited by a constant nostalgia for 'the sun, beaches and islands where the trade winds blow', and by the 'youth whose memory drives him to despair'. He could very well have been one of the characters who illustrated the duality which runs through Camus's last published work, *L'Exil et le royaume*, in the same way as it had dominated *L'Envers et l'endroit* in 1938. He too experiences the conflict between life in society and the kingdom which lies immediately to hand, for the young at any rate, in the world of nature. Part of the appeal of Camus's work, as I argued in the discussion of *L'Etranger*, lies in the expression which it gives to a certain number of myths. One of the most powerful of these, and one which underlines how very closely linked Camus's work is to the Romantic movement, is the conviction that almost all forms of society are somehow bad.

Meursault, it is true, is quite at home in his own fairly small social sub-group. The people who know him find him quite acceptable, and there is no doubt about the feelings which he inspires in Marie. But as soon as his crime brings him into contact

with society at large, the possibility of anyone understanding him
totally disappears. In *La Peste*, it is the smallness of Tarrou's
'équipes sanitaires' which makes them so attractive. Society
as a whole is represented either by a totally impersonal
administration, or by the indifference to anything other than
short-term commercial interests which characterises the mass of
the inhabitants of Oran, or by lawyers such as Tarrou's father or
Judge Othon. The workshop in which Yvars has previously been
so happy exercising his individual skill is a small one, and
Camus's account of it has almost a touch of the idealisation of the
shepherd and the artisan in the literature of English as well as
French Romanticism.

This aspect of Camus's appeal is even more visible if you look at
the attitude to language which runs through almost all his fiction.
The only character in the short stories who does not seem to have
any kind of authentic kingdom is the loquacious narrator in *Le
Renégat ou l'esprit confus*, and it is easy to see why: he is too much a
man of ideas and of language ever to escape from the exile which
his preoccupation with both of them has forced upon him. Like
Clamence, another man of words, he also worships power. Not
long after he has been taken prisoner, he switches from the
Christianity which he thought was going to enable him to rule
over the savages to the worship of the fetish which has now
enslaved him. As the words of his monologue run unceasingly
through his head, he is waiting to shoot down the missionary who
has been sent to take his place. He does not succeed, and the story
ends as 'a mouthful of sand fills the mouth of the talkative
slave'.[142]

The characters in his fiction for whom Camus invites us to feel
the least sympathy are indeed those who make too easy a use of
language: the prosecuting counsel in Meursault's trial; the
Paneloux of the first sermon in *La Peste*; Tarrou's father; the
Clamence of *La Chute*; and the failed missionary in *L'Esprit confus*.
The quality in Meursault which his friends most appreciate is the
fact that he doesn't talk very much, and this could again be an
autobiographical touch. Camus noted in his *Carnets* for 1942 that
'three people entered into the making of *L'Etranger*: two men (of
whom one was myself) and one woman',[143] and one of the essays
in *L'Envers et l'endroit* describes him sitting for long periods quite
silently with his mother. But although this enviable taciturnity is a
slightly curious theme to find in the books of a man whose use of

language has given so much pleasure to so many people, it is not inconsistent with the attempt which runs through all his work to construct a particular kind of value system.

This attempt is most visible in *L'Etranger* and *La Peste*, and may well account for the fact that it is these books which have sold the most copies. It is also in these two novels that Camus expresses his most powerful myths, and it is the combination between these two aspects of his work – the conscious quest for values and the less conscious myth-making – which constitutes one of his major contributions to the achievements and world of the modern novel. In *L'Etranger*, the dominant myth is at first sight a paradoxical one: although the world has no ultimate meaning, and can on occasion be the very opposite of providential, it is nevertheless a place in which certain men can be granted the grace of feeling absolutely at home. This accounts, as I have argued, for the continuity in appeal of *L'Etranger* from the poverty-stricken forties to the affluent sixties and beyond.

The second, more rationalistic appeal of *L'Etranger* is perhaps best illustrated by a remark which Jean-Paul Sartre made in the article which he wrote in 1950 to mark the death of André Gide. He said there that one of the major reasons for Gide's importance as a thinker lay in his decision to 'live through the death and death agony of God'.[144] It is a remark which could be equally well applied to the whole of Camus's work. At a period in which religious faith, certainly is measured by empty churches and the virtual disappearance of candidates for the priesthood, is declining more rapidly than at any time in European history, Camus's approach to the problems and possibilities opened up by an almost universal agnosticism makes him into one of the leading novelists of the age of unbelief. This is one of the reasons why he is so interesting.

What he tried to put in the place of the traditional values of Christianity, at least in *L'Etranger*, was a cult of personal honesty. I have argued in Chapter 2 that this was not an entirely satisfactory solution, at least as far as the character of Meursault is concerned. It is another sign of Camus's links with Romanticism that his hero should be at one and the same time so attractive and yet so vulnerable to rational analysis. This, again, is a characteristic of the myth, and Camus's contribution to the development of the Romantic figure of the outsider is an involuntary acknowledgement of how difficult it is, on aesthetic as well as philosophical grounds, to use fiction to assert moral values. Had Meursault been what Camus claimed he was in his 1955 preface, the austere new hero of our godless age, he might also have been a bit of a bore. As it is, his communion with the natural world gives him a permanent attraction in a world in which the growth of leisure offers more opportunities than at any time in history for swimming and sunbathing. At the same time, Meursault's very ambivalent attitude to rationally formulated concepts of truth endows him with two additional advantages: it gives him an attractively human inconsistency; it makes him a perfect hero for the rebels against middle-class society who want to have their cake and eat it. For he is, and is likely to remain, the perfect incarnation of the essentially Romantic view that personal integrity is impossible in middle-class society.

L'Etranger continues the Romantic tradition through the creation of a character who at one and the same time incarnates a myth and sets an insoluble intellectual problem. He is not, nor is he likely to be, as inexhaustibly fascinating as Prince Hamlet. You would not want to dine with him more than once. But he is in the same league as the Julien Sorel of Stendhal's *Le Rouge et le Noir*: the sexually attractive young man in conflict with a rather dull society. He is different from Julien in that he does not try to impose himself on this society. He lacks the driving force which enables you to see why both Madame de Rênal and Mathilde de La Môle find Stendhal's hero so attractive. But he is like Julien in the enmity he arouses and in the inevitability with which everything he does is made to lead to his death. He is also, like Julien, a working-class hero. Although Camus made no deliberate attempt to use his own very unusual personal career as subject matter for his fiction, he gave all his characters an identifiable place in society. You know what they do for a living. Meursault is a clerk in an office, not a rather vague embodiment of a set of philosophical problems.

One of the great advantages of Camus as a writer of ideas is that his characters are brought face to face with their destiny as a result of what they do for a living. In the case of Rieux, as in that of Clamence, their job makes it impossible to elude the moral and philosophical problems which they then have to try to solve. 'I have spent too long in hospitals to believe in the idea of collective punishment'[145] is one of the several remarks by which Rieux provides Paneloux with an unanswerable objection to one of the priest's theories, and it is through the character of Rieux that Camus's humanism is stated in its most convincing form. In 1955, Camus wrote a long preface to the 'Pléiade' edition of the works of another French author to have won the Nobel Prize for literature, Roger Martin du Gard. One of the most interesting of Martin du Gard's characters, Antoine Thibault, is also a doctor, and is made to voice very much the same objections to Christianity as Dr Rieux. Neither he nor Rieux can accept that a world in which physical pain is so universal an experience, and in which it so often serves no detectable purpose, can possibly stem from the hand of God.

In this respect, Camus is in the humanist tradition of Matthew Arnold, George Eliot and Bertrand Russell, and there are also times when his work recalls the preoccupations of Aldous Huxley. He does not, it is true, go so far as to create a character who, like Spandrell in *Point Counter Point*, asks whether this world might not be another planet's hell. Although his themes may link him to the Romantic tradition, his mode of expression constantly avoids the hysterical. But *La Peste* nevertheless echoes one of the ideas which Huxley put into the mouth of the Fifth Earl of Hauberk in *After Many a Summer* in 1939:

> The Christians talk much of Pain, but nothing of what they say is to the point. For the most remarkable Characteristics of Pain are these: the Disproportion between the enormity of physical suffering and its often trifling causes; and the manner in which, by annihilating every faculty and reducing the body to helplessness, it defeats the Object for which it was apparently devised by Nature: viz. to warn the sufferer of the approach of Danger, whether from within or without. In relation to Pain, that empty word, Infinity, comes near to having a meaning.[146]

Like Huxley, Camus is a novelist of ideas. As such, he has played something of the same role in the intellectual development of young people in the second half of the twentieth century as Huxley did from the 1930s to the 1950s. Not only is this a most honourable role for the novelist to fulfil. There is also a sense in which Camus does it rather better than Huxley, while at the same time offering an interesting challenge to Dostoevsky, Tolstoy or George Eliot. He may lack Huxley's intellectual range, and the ability to make the reader feel almost as clever as the characters in the novel. But his novels are in a totally different league as far as style and structure are concerned. Because of Camus's taste for a mode of writing in which experience is brought under rational control, they are almost entirely free of digressions. This makes them, for the modern reader, more immediately accessible than the work of the great nineteenth-century writers who also used the novel for the presentation and exploration of moral and philosophical ideas. What Camus's fiction shows is that you can combine an interest in ideas with an almost puritanical awareness of form.

It is true that *La Peste* is not so rigorously constructed as *L'Etranger* and *La Chute*. It is also true that Camus writes better in the borrowed voice of Meursault or of Clamence than he does when the looser form of the chronicle no longer obliges him to stick to one particular mode of expression. Clamence's monologue, which is at one and the same time a *plaidoirie* and a *réquisitoire*, shows the same kind of ability to speak through an assumed voice as the two sermons in *La Peste*, the monologue in *L'Esprit confus* or the very particular style in which Meursault tells his own story. This ability may well have been linked to Camus's interest in the stage, and is an interesting reflection on how literary ambitions sometimes end up by fulfilling themselves in an indirect and unintended form. Both *L'Etranger* and *La Chute* remind us of the theatre at the same time as they illustrate how right W. H. Auden was when he wrote that 'the truest poetry is the most feigning'.

The style that Camus chose when he wanted to express what he personally thought and felt was a peculiarly French combination of lyricism and rhetoric. The two authors it most recalled were Barrès and Chateaubriand. 'Je ne vous reproche pas votre pompe, qui vous est naturelle' (I won't criticise you for your tendency to pomposity, which comes naturally to you), wrote Sartre rather cruelly in his open letter to Camus in August 1952,[147] and you can perhaps see even more clearly what he meant if your native language is English. The cult of plain speech and ordinary language which has characterised some poets and many philosophers in mid-twentieth-century England has not had its counterpart on the other other side of the Channel. The more rhetorical style which has remained in fashion there gives the Camus of *L'Homme révolté*, and even of certain pages of *Noces*, a rather forced sound to the ear of the native English speaker. This has the additional effect of making Camus's ideas seem more unusual than they actually are, and it may even explain some of the hostility which his political stance evoked during his lifetime in France itself. He was, after Gide and Malraux, the third major French writer to turn against Communism, and the publication of *L'Homme révolté* in 1951 aroused passions which now seem a little misplaced. Virtually everything that Camus said in that book was to become commonplace in the Paris of the late 1970s, and there is remarkably little in André Glucksmann's *Les Maîtres penseurs* or Bernard-Henri Lévy's *La Barbarie à visage humain* which Camus had not written almost thirty years earlier. All three authors agree in seeing Communism as a systematic attempt to take people's liberty from them. Each blames Marx for arguing that since history will inevitably produce the classless society, anybody who opposes this historical process deserves nothing but elimination. All three see Soviet Russia as a complete perversion of the original socialist desire to produce a society in which men will be free and equal. The unpopularity which Camus achieved by putting forward these three unimpeachable theses in the Paris of the 1950s was partly due to the fact that he was, in France, ahead of his time. But it was also a by-product of his decision to write what was in fact a work of political analysis in so highly formal and rhetorical a style.

There are times when even the dialogues in *La Peste* strike the English-speaking reader as a shade too highflown, and it is perhaps Camus's least successful novel from a purely formal point of view. It is also, by the same token, the most obviously sincere, in the sense of most clearly expressing what he personally thought and felt. It may consequently keep its place as one of his most popular works, especially as far as sales figures are concerned. However much literary critics like to insist on the idea of a watertight compartment separating the man who lived from the author who wrote, most ordinary readers like to think that a writer is talking about his own experiences and expressing his own view of the world. This is especially the case with an author such as Camus, whose own life was so unusual, whose personality seemed so attractive, and whose ideas struck so deep a chord in so many people. One should certainly try to look at Camus in the terms that he preferred, as 'an objective writer . . . who chooses themes without ever taking himself as subject'.[148] But there will always be a sense in which he seems, as a man, to have been more interesting than any one of his literary works. There is no reason why his novels should not therefore be read in the code which so many readers enjoy, that of a series of autobiographical fragments, each marking a different stage in his own intellectual development.

The intensity of the isolated young man's rejection of all conventional values in *L'Etranger* is followed by the more adult quest for a code of ethical conduct involving other people in *La Peste*. This, in turn, is followed by the anguished self-doubt of *La Chute*, an almost perfect translation into fictional form of the moment in a man's life when, like the Narrator in Dante's *Inferno*, he reaches the middle years and finds the straight path hidden. Where he would have gone after the experiments in narrative technique and the exploration of the more private problems of human existence in *L'Exil et le royaume* is impossible to say.

Notes

1 THE MAN, THE BOOKS AND THE THEMES

1. P_{II} 20.
2. P_{II} 25.
3. C_{II} 178.
4. The details about Camus's early life are drawn partly from Herbert Lottman's *Albert Camus. A Biography* (London: Weidenfeld and Nicolson, 1979), and partly from conversation with people who knew him.
5. P_{II} 65.
6. C_{II} 124.
7. P_{II} 357.
8. The full text of this broadcast is in P_I 1718–26.
9. Interview in *La Gazette des Lettres*, 15 February 1952, reprinted in Jean-Claude Brisville, *Camus*, La Bibliothèque Idéale (Paris: Gallimard, 1952), and in P_{II} 1919–24.
10. These two reviews were reprinted in P_{II} 1417–22. See also *LC* and *SEN*.
11. See *Combat*, 10 December 1944.
12. P_{II} 1783.
13. See Lottman, p. 618. For a further explanation of what Camus meant, see P_{II} 1882 for a letter which he wrote to *Le Monde* on 13 December 1958. In 1958, in his *Avant-Propos* to *Actuelles III*, his own selection of articles on Algeria which he called *Chroniques algériennes*, he also wrote: 'For my own part, if I am aware of the risk I run, by criticising the way the rebellion has developed, of giving a fatally easy conscience to those who have the longest and most insolent responsibility for the Algeria drama [PT: presumably the richer of the European settlers] I never cease to be afraid what I might, by outlining the long succession of French mistakes, provide without any risk for myself an alibi to the criminal lunatic who will throw his bomb into an innocent crowd containing some of my family' (P_{II} 892).
14. P_{II} 894.
15. The articles entitled *Ni victimes ni bourreaux* were republished in *Actuelles I* (Paris: Gallimard, 1950), as well as in P_{II}. A number of them were included in *RRD*.
16. See P_{II} 1016. Jonathan King's edition of Camus's *Selected Political Writings* (London: Methuen, 1981) is a most useful way of studying Camus's attitude to the Algerian problem, as well as his views on other political issues.

113

17. Pɪɪ 896.

18. Pɪɪ 1059. The full English text is in *RRD*, as well as in the volume originally published by Koestler and Camus in 1957.

2 TECHNIQUE, CODES AND AMBIGUITY

19. For details of *Le Premier homme*, see Lottman, p. 7. Camus is not the only French writer to have lost his father when he was still very young. Roland Barthes, Charles Baudelaire, Alexandre Dumas *père*, Jean Genet, André Gide, François Mauriac, Charles Péguy, Antoine de Saint-Exupéry, Jean-Paul Sartre and Emile Zola all lost their fathers well before puberty. Rousseau and Stendhal were *orphelins de mère* when still babies. The greatest of all French writers, Jean Racine, had lost both father and mother by the age of three.

20. *Point Counter Point* (London: Chatto and Windus, 1928), pp. 409–10.

21. For the figures of Camus's and other authors' sales, see *Quid*, 1985 (Paris: Robert Laffont), p. 297.

22. Pɪ 1887–93 and *LC* 153–7. See also *SEN* 185–91.

23. Pɪɪ 659.

24. *C*ɪɪ 89.

25. *C*ɪɪ 337.

26. See Pɪɪ 1417, *LC* 145 and *SEN* 167.

27. Pɪ 1354.

28. See *Situations I* (Paris: Gallimard, 1947), p. 7.

29. For Paratoud, see *Confluences*, No. 3 (1942), 209–10.

For the *NRF* review, see No. 343 (September 1942), 329–31.

For Wyndham Lewis, see *The Writer and the Absolute* (London: Methuen, 1952), p. 87.

For Nathan A. Scott, see his *Camus*, Studies in Modern European Literature and Thought (London: Bowes and Bowes, 1962), p. 37.

For a comparable view of *L'Etranger* as a novel expressing 'the disappearance of what was specifically human in man', see Pierre Lafue, 'Nouveaux psychologues', in *Problèmes du Roman*, edited by Jean Prévost (Brussels: Editions Le Carrefour, 1945), pp. 168–70.

For a discussion of other contemporary reactions to *L'Etranger*, see *C*ɪɪ 189–91.

For a fuller account of other interpretations of *L'Etranger*, see *Cahiers Albert Camus*, v (Paris: Gallimard, 1982). This volume is especially interesting for the reproduction of a long talk given by Alain Robbe-Grillet (pp. 215–27) in which he argues that the only worthwhile part of Camus's work is in the first four chapters of *L'Etranger*. After that, what Robbe-Grillet calls 'humanism' creeps in and spoils everything. He thus repeated, in 1982, the same views which he had expressed in 1958 in an article entitled 'Nature, humanisme, tragédie', republished in *Pour un nouveau roman*, Collection Idées (Paris: Gallimard, 1963): that any attempt to describe the world in human terms is a distortion of reality; that the personalisation of nature which is evident in the increasingly frequent metaphors in *L'Etranger* is a deplorable falling away from the totally neutral description of objects in the first few pages; and that *L'Etranger* is not as good a book as some people have thought because of the 'fatal complicity' with the world implied by its metaphors. In May 1940, after he had read George Orwell's essay on *Boys' Weeklies*, Frank Richards commented on some of the presuppositions which Orwell had found running through *The Gem* and *The Magnet*. 'As for foreigners being funny,' he wrote, 'I must shock Mr Orwell by telling him that foreigners *are* funny.' See *The Collected Essays, Journalism and Letters of George Orwell*, I (London: Secker and Warburg, 1968), p. 491.

30. See *L'Arche*, No. 5 (1944), 115–17, 'Sur le sentiment d'étrangeté'.

31. PI 1164 and Laredo 47.

32. See *Scrutiny*, XIV, No. 2 (December 1946), 84. Champigny's book was published by Gallimard, Paris, in 1959.

33. PI 1149.

34. Interview in *Le Littéraire* (subsequently *Le Figaro Littéraire*), 10 August 1946. For the letter to Rousseaux, see CII 29–30.

35. CII 32–3 for the reference to Ulysses. See PII 39 for the quotation from *L'Envers et l'endroit*.

36. PII 64 and 67.

37. For the lecture by John Weightman, see *Encounter*, December 1970, 9–18. For Camus's view, see PII 69 and *LC* 63.

38. Camus on Gide: PII 69.

39. PII 72; *LC* 67. For Céleste as one of Camus's favourite characters (the other two are Dora in *Les Justes* and Maria in *Le Malentendu*) see J.-C. Brisville, *Camus*, p. 258.

40. PI 1197.

41. See *L'Etranger*, edited by Germaine Brée and Carlos Lynes (London: Methuen, 1958). Camus's preface is also translated as an *Afterword* to Joseph Laredo's 1981 translation, as well as in *LC* and *SEN*.

42. PI 1154.

43. See CII 41 for public library. See *Albert Camus, 1913–1960* (Edisud, 1981), p. 23. Catalogue of an exhibition held at the University of Nice, 8–14 May 1980 and at the *Centre Georges Pompidou*, 25 March–4 May 1981.

44. See *Situations I*, pp. 101–2.

45. PII 150. When I discussed Camus's work with him in August 1956, he drew my attention to the applicability of this sentence to the character of Meursault. He also said that Meursault was to be seen as having gone through the experience of discovering the absurd before the action of *L'Etranger* begins.

46. PII 142–4.

47. Interview in *Les Nouvelles Littéraires*, 15 November 1945. PII 1426. *EN* 261. In the collection of essays entitled *Pour un nouveau roman*, p. 50, Alain Robbe-Grillet argues that if you were to change the tenses in *L'Etranger*, the whole of Camus's world would disappear.

48. See *Albert Camus and the Literature of Revolt* (Oxford University Press, 1959), p. 162.

49. Herbert Rumpole is a somewhat down-at-heel English barrister, the invention of the playwright John Mortimer. Rumpole never prosecutes and is successful in bringing off some remarkable acquittals. When, in 1982, John Mortimer published his autobiography, *Clinging to the Wreckage*, he prefaced it with the following quotation from Justin O'Brien's translation of *Le Mythe de Sisyphe*: 'For the absurd man, it is not a matter of explaining and solving but of experiencing and describing. Everything begins with a lucid indifference.'

50. PI 1203. Laredo 88–9.

51. See *The Verbal Ikon* (1954; Kentucky Paperbacks, University of Kentucky Press, 1967). Camus's preface and interviews make it impossible to observe the injunction on p. 5 that 'We ought to impute the thoughts and attitudes of the poem immediately to the dramatic *speaker*, and if to the author at all, only by an act of biographical inference.'

52. *C*ɪɪ 177. Roger Quilliot, who was a close friend of Camus's and edited both volumes in the Pléiade edition of his work, told me in private conversation that Camus was a great admirer of d'Aubigné (1552–1630), a staunch defender of Protestantism.

53. *C*ɪɪ 317.

54. See Lottman, p. 207 and Ghani Merad's article, '*L'Etranger* de Camus vu sous un angle psychosociologique', *Revue Romane*, No. 10 (1975), 61.

55. Conor Cruise O'Brien, *Camus*, Fontana Modern Masters (London: Fontana/Collins, 1970), p. 27. For Henri Kréa, see 'Le malentendu algérien', on p. 16 of *France-Observateur*, No. 557 (5 January 1961). In an accompanying article, Pierre Nora argued that the execution of Meursault, 'far from evoking some Kafka-like "Trial", is the disturbing confession of a historical guilt, and takes on the appearance of an anticipatory tragedy'. See below, note 57, for a comparable view.

56. *La Nef*, November 1957, 95.

57. The interpretation of *L'Etranger* as an unconsciously racialist book was severely criticised in a number of articles published in the 1972 issue of *Revue des Lettres Modernes*, nos. 315–22. On pp. 178–87, André Abbou maintained that the large number of minor errors in Conor Cruise O'Brien's book prevented it from being taken seriously as a study of Camus's work. He also argued that O'Brien was projecting on to Camus his own obsessions, as an Irishman, with British imperialism. On pp. 275–8, Jean Gassin suggested that this aspect of *L'Etranger* was a conscious and deliberate unmasking by Camus of the colonialist reality in Algeria.

58. See *Camus* (New Brunswick: Rutgers University Press, 1959), p. 114.

59. See *The Unique Creation of Albert Camus*, p. 89. There is no evidence that Mr Lazere is trying to be funny.

60. *Situations I*, p. 71.

61. *P*ɪɪ 1685.

3 EVIL, ALLEGORY AND REVOLT

62. See *P*ɪɪ 813–32. *LC* 85–103. *CEN* 105–24.

63. *Les Conquérants*, 1928. The quotation is on p. 57 of the 1954 Livre de Poche edition in which Garine writes: 'Je ne tiens pas la société pour mauvaise, pour susceptible d'être améliorée; je la tiens pour absurde.'

64. For A. J. Ayer's comments on Sartre and Camus, see *Horizon*, March 1946, 155–66.

65. *P*ɪ 1272–4. For the actual format of the cards by which the French were allowed to communicate in 1940, see Henri Amouroux, *La Grande Histoire des Français sous l'Occupation*, ɪɪ, *Quarante millions de Pétainistes* (Paris: Robert Laffont, 1977), p. 146.

66. *P*ɪ 1899–1903. *LC* 205–9. *SEN* 178–82.

67. Pɪ 1978. Perhaps because of the seriousness with which he discusses religious problems, Camus has proved very attractive to Christian thinkers. One of his best-informed critics, however, Thomas Hanna, wrote in his article 'Camus and the Christian faith', *The Journal of Religion*, xxxvi, No. 4 (October 1956), 230: 'It is a curious thing about the thought of Albert Camus that he has not estranged himself from Christian readers. This may possibly be because Christian thinkers have not as yet realised the full import of what he has said about the Christian faith.'

68. On 9 February 1941, Maurras published an article in *Le Petit Marseillais* actually entitled 'La divine surprise' (see Jean-Louis Azéma, *De Munich à la Libération* (Paris: Editions du Seuil, 1979), p. 102). However, according to Henri Amouroux (p. 263), Maurras was already writing in 1940 that it was 'grâce au ciel' that the French had been delivered from the evils of parliamentary democracy. At his trial, in 1945, Maurras observed that the phrase 'le miracle Pétain' had originally been pronounced by Pope Pius XII (Amouroux, p. 280). See ending to note 29 above.

69. Amouroux, v, *Les Passions et les haines* (Paris: Laffont, 1981), p. 331. Azéma, p. 209.

70. Pɪ 1401. *CF* 201.

71. Cɪɪ 66. For Christianity as a doctrine of injustice, see *La Remarque sur la révolte*, Pɪɪ 1690. For a further discussion of the concept of revolt in Christian thought, see the opening chapters of *L'Homme révolté*, Pɪɪ 435–46.

72. Cɪɪ 129.

73. Interview with Jeanine Delpech, *Les Nouvelles Littéraires*, 15 November 1945. Pɪɪ 1424–7. *LC* 259–61.

74. Pɪɪ 123.

75. See *Pensées*, Lafuma edition, No. 182. Camus discussed Pascal's wager argument in an essay entitled 'Sur une philosophie de l'expression', *Poésie*, xLIV (1944). See Pɪɪ 1671–82, especially 1676.

76. Pɪ 1321. *CF* 144.

77. Brochier (Paris: Editions André Balland), 1979, *passim*.

78. Barthes, '*La Peste*: annales d'une épidémie ou roman de la solitude', *Club*, February 1955, pp. 4–6. Camus's reply is in Pɪ 1965–6 and in *LC* and *SEN*.

79. Sartre, *Situations IV* (Paris: Gallimard, 1962), p. 118. This article, 'Réponse à Albert Camus', originally appeared in *Les Temps Modernes* in August 1952, and was Sartre's principal contribution to the argument about *L'Homme révolté*.

80. Pɪ 1172. Pɪɪ 1420. *LC* 148. *SEN* 170.

81. Cɪɪ 325.

82. Pɪɪ 1424. *CF* 218.

83. Pɪɪ 1424. *CF* 218.

84. For Eichmann, see Hannah Arendt, *Eichmann in Jerusalem: A Report on the Banality of Evil* (New York: Random House, Viking Press, 1964), pp. 5, 287. For Steiner, see *The Portage to San Cristobal of A.H.* (London: Faber Paperbacks, 1981), p. 125, Hitler's closing speech: 'Ribbentrop told me: of the man's [Stalin's] contempt for *us*. Whom he found contemptible, corrupt with mercy. Our terrors were village carnivals compared to his; he had strung wire and death pits around a continent.'

85. Arendt, p. 105.

86. See *Orwell, Collected Essays, Journalism and Letters*, IV p. 136.
87. See *The Observer*, 2 February 1966. C_{II} 154.
88. See his reply to Roland Barthes, P_I 1965–6. *LC* 253–5. *SEN* 220–2.
89. P_I 1329. *CF* 150.
90. P_{II} 1692.
91. *Combat*, 24 November 1944. P_{II} 282.
92. For Wollheim, see *Cambridge Journal*, October 1953, 3–19. Camus had a copy of *The Open Society and its Enemies* on his bookshelves in his Paris flat in the rue Madame.
93. P_I 1325. *CF* 147.
94. This reading of the 1962 missile crisis, including the phrase about 'a side-arm persuader', was suggested to me by a senior Canadian diplomat who was in Moscow at the time and knew Krushchev well. It has the advantage of fitting the facts.
95. Simone de Beauvoir, *La Force des choses* (Paris: Gallimard, 1963), p. 250.
96. See note 12 to Chapter 1.
97. P_{II} 1013. This quotation, from p. 203 of the original Gallimard edition of *Actuelles III*, was picked out and quoted by Henri Kréa in his article 'Le malentendu algérien', *France-Observateur*, 5 January 1961, as further proof of the right-wing nature of Camus's thought.
98. For Camus's views on Dostoevsky, see P_I 1877–80.
99. P_I 1324. *CF* 146.
100. P_I 1467. *CF* 246.
101. *Œuvres complètes*, Pléiade (Paris: Gallimard, 1963), p. 877. From 'A quoi bon la critique?', *Salon de 1846*.
102. P_I 1309. *CF* 135.
103. P_I 1463. *CF* 243.
104. P_{II} 413.

4 LAWYERS, GUILT AND SATIRE

105. This point was originally made by Sartre, in 1944. See *Situations I*, p. 116. A Voltairean note is especially visible on P_I 1170, Laredo 53.
106. P_I 1299, 1415, 1499.
107. P_I 1482.
108. P_I 1545.
109. Lottman, p. 83.
110. P_I 1518. Lottman, p. 40. See also *The Joy of Football*, by Brian Glanville (London: Hodder and Stoughton, 1986), for a longer quotation of Camus's remarks.
111. P_{II} 869, 874–5. *LC* 122, 131. P_I 1487.
112. P_{II} 879. P_I 1499.
113. *Polyeucte*, act IV, scene 3, line 1268.
114. He referred to him in 1944 in an essay entitled *Sur une philosophie de l'expression*, originally published in *Poésie* and reprinted in P_{II} 1671–82. Although he is talking about Pascal's attitude to language, the vocabulary he uses to discuss him on 1676 is very similar to that of *Le Mythe de Sisyphe* and of Paneloux's second sermon: 'This is why Pascal suggests not a solution but a submission.

Submission to traditional language because it comes to us from God, humility in the face of words in order to find out their true inspiration. We have to choose between miracles and absurdity, there is no middle way. We know the choice Pascal made.' See *LC* 160–9. Later in the same article (P$_{II}$ 1678–9; *LC* 166), he quotes Parain as saying that any philosophy which does not refute Pascal is useless, and adds: 'This is true, even for minds which nothing predisposes towards miracles.'

115. See *Situations IV*, p. 127. The article originally appeared in *France-Observateur* on 7 January 1960, after Camus's death.

116. Adèle King, *Camus* (Edinburgh: Oliver and Boyd, 1964), p. 91.

117. P$_{I}$ 1490, 1502.

118. P$_{I}$ 1207.

119. Orwell, *Collected Essays, Journalism and Letters*, III, p. 175 and IV, pp. 68–9: 'Prose literature as we know it is the product of rationalism, of the Protestant centuries, of the autonomous individual.'

120. O'Brien, pp. 81 and 91.

121. C$_{II}$ 317.

122. See P$_{I}$ 2002 and 2006.

123. P$_{I}$ 1487.

124. Brisville, *Camus*, p. 259.

125. P$_{II}$ 475 and 477: 'Whatever some Christian critics may believe, Nietzsche did not form the project of killing God. He found Him dead in the soul of his time.'

126. P$_{I}$ 2002.

127. See Sartre, *Saint Genet, comédien et martyr* (Gallimard, 1952), pp. 517–23.

128. *Situations IV*, p. 108.

129. For Clamence, see P$_{I}$ 1535. For the letter to P.B., see P$_{II}$ 2050–3. Also *LC* and *SEN*.

130. For Clamence, see P$_{I}$ 1502. For Camus's *Avant-Propos*, see P$_{II}$ 898.

5 EXILE, HUMANISM AND A CONCLUSION

131. P$_{II}$ 72. *LC* 66. *SEN* 86.

132. C$_{II}$ 345.

133. See *La Nef*, November 1957, 95.

134. *CI* 1636.

135. P$_{II}$ 1080–1. Camus's Nobel Prize speeches were translated by Justin O'Brien and reprinted in *Resistance, Rebellion and Death*.

136. For Derrida, see *Philosophy and Literature*, edited by A. Phillips Griffiths (Cambridge: Cambridge University Press, 1984), p. 187.

137. P$_{II}$ 167, P$_{I}$ 1465.

138. Brisville, p. 256.

139. P$_{II}$ 57. See also *LC* and *SEN*.

140. P$_{I}$ 1560.

141. P$_{I}$ 1573.

142. P$_{I}$ 1591.

143. C$_{II}$ 34.

144. *Situations IV*, p. 88.

145. Pɪ 1319.
146. *After Many a Summer*, Collected Fiction of Aldous Huxley (London: Chatto and Windus, 1947), p. 257.
147. *Situations IV*, p. 97.
148. Pɪɪ 864. From an essay entitled *L'Enigme*, originally written in 1950 and published in book form in *L'Eté* in 1954. See also *LC*.

Bibliography and References

Except for *La Mort heureuse*, which was published separately in 1971 (Paris: Gallimard) and translated by Richard Howard in 1972 (London: Hamish Hamilton; New York: Knopf), all Camus's plays, fiction and major essays are available in two volumes in the Gallimard 'Pléiade' series. The first (1962) includes the plays, novels, and texts relating to Camus's work as an imaginative writer. The second (1965) includes his essays and a wide selection of his journalism. The first volume of his *Carnets*, covering the period 1935–42, was published by Gallimard in 1962; the second, covering the period 1942–51, in 1965. His correspondence with Jean Grenier was published by Gallimard in 1981.

In addition to *La Mort heureuse*, which appeared in 1971 as the first of the *Cahiers Albert Camus*, there have been four issues in the same series:

Journaux de Voyage, edited by Roger Quilliot (Gallimard, 1978). This contains Camus's account of his visit to North America in March 1946 and to South America in 1949.

Fragments d'un combat (two volumes, dealing with Camus's work on *Alger Républicain* and *Le Soir Républicain* between 1938 and 1940), edited by Jacqueline Lévi-Valensi and André Abbou (Gallimard, 1978).

'*Caligula*', version de 1941, suivi de la poétique du premier '*Caligula*', edited by A. James Arnold (Gallimard, 1984).

Œuvre fermée, œuvre ouverte. Actes du Colloque du Centre Culturel de Cérisy-la-Salle, juin 1982, edited by Raymond Gay-Croisier and Jacqueline Lévi-Valensi (Gallimard, 1985).

Except for *L'Etranger*, where I have used the revised translation by Joseph Laredo (London: Hamish Hamilton, 1981), I have used the translation published in 1960 by Hamish Hamilton of

121

The Collected Fiction of Albert Camus. A selection of Camus's political essays, translated by Justin O'Brien, was published in 1960 under the title of *Resistance, Rebellion and Death* (London: Hamish Hamilton; New York: Knopf). A translation of *Noces, L'Envers et l'endroit* and *L'Eté*, together with essays on René Char, William Faulkner, Roger Martin du Gard, André Gide, Jean Grenier, Brice Parain, Jules Roy, Ignazio Silone and Jean-Paul Sartre, was published under the title *Lyrical and Critical* in 1967 by Hamish Hamilton, London, and Knopf, New York. This volume also contains three interviews by Camus, together with texts on *L'Etranger* and *La Chute.* In 1971, the Penguin edition of Camus's *Selected Essays and Notebooks* reprinted the translation of *Noces, L'Envers et l'endroit* and *L'Eté*, together with a number of Camus's critical essays and a selection from the two volumes of his *Carnets.*

Both volumes of the *Carnets* have been published in translation, in 1963 and 1966 respectively, by Hamish Hamilton, London, and Knopf, New York. They contain notes linking the entries to Camus's other books, to events in his life, to his political views and to his reading.

There is a great deal of critical writing on Camus. The *Revue des Lettres Modernes* publishes regular special numbers on him. These contain a full account of recently published work. Editions for use in schools are available of all his major novels and plays. Those published by Methuen, London, all have a full critical bibliography.

Most of the major critical works on Camus are mentioned below in the Notes. Readers interested in following up some of the ideas in Donald Lazere's *The Unique Creation of Albert Camus* (New Haven and London: Yale University Press, 1973) will find Léon Coste's *Albert Camus ou la parole manquante* (Paris: Payot, 1973) equally instructive. John Cruickshank's *Albert Camus and the Literature of Revolt* (Oxford University Press, 1959) remains one of the best studies of Camus within the English literary and philosophical tradition. Camus's relationship with Christianity has been especially well studied by Thomas Hanna in *The Thought and Art of Albert Camus* (Chicago: Henry Regnery Company, 1958); by Jean Onimus in the series 'Les Ecrivains devant Dieu' (Paris: Desclée et Brouwer, 1965); and by Bruce Pratt in *L'Evangile selon Albert Camus* (Paris: Joseph Corti, 1980). Camus's political activity and ideas are presented in Emmett Parker's *Albert Camus. The Artist in the Arena* (Madison and Milwaukee: University of

Wisconsin Press, 1965); in Eric Werner's *De la violence au totalitarisme. Essai sur la pensée de Camus et de Sartre* (Paris: Calmann-Lévy, 1972); and in Susan Tarrow's *Exile from the Kingdom: A Political Re-Reading of Albert Camus* (University of Alabama Press, 1985). Jonathan King's selection of Camus's *Selected Political Writings* (London: Methuen Educational, 1981) also has an excellent set of notes on the political background.

Readers wishing to see a more detailed application of Conor Cruise O'Brien's approach in his 1970 'Fontana Modern Masters' volume will find it in Patrick McCarthy's *Camus. A Critical Study of his Life and Work* (London: Hamish Hamilton, 1982). Readers interested in knowing what Camus looked like will find a number of photographs in Morvan Lebesque, *Camus par lui-même*, 'Ecrivains de toujours' (Paris: Editions du Seuil, 1963) and in the splendid volume entitled *Camus* published in the Hachette 'Génies et réalités' series in 1964.

The following abbreviations are used in the Notes:

PI   – Pléiade I, *Théâtre, récits, nouvelles*
PII – Pléiade II, *Essais*
CI   – *Carnets 1935–42*
CII – *Carnets 1942–51*
CF   – *Collected Fiction of Albert Camus*
Laredo – *The Outsider*, translated by Joseph Laredo, 1981
RRD – *Resistance, Rebellion and Death*
LC   – *Lyrical and Critical*
SEN – *Selected Essays and Notebooks*

Index